The Urhobo Language Today

The Urhobo Language Today

edited by

Tanure Ojaide, PhD
Professor of African-American and African Studies at the University of North Carolina at Charlotte
&
Rose Aziza, PhD
Head of Department of Languages and Linguistics and Director of the Urhobo Studies Programme at Delta State University, Abraka, Nigeria

malthouse ⋊ₚ

Malthouse Press Limited
Lagos, Benin, Ibadan, Jos, Oxford, Zaria

Malthouse Press Limited
43 Onitana Street, Off Stadium Hotel Road
Surulere, Lagos
E-mail: malthouse_press@yahoo.com
Tel: 01-773 53 44; 0802 364 2402

Lagos Benin Ibadan Jos Port Harcourt Zaria

All rights reserved. No part of this publication may be reproduced, transmitted, transcribed, stored in a retrieval system or translated into any language or computer language, in any form or by any means, electronic, mechanical, magnetic, chemical, thermal, manual or otherwise, without the prior consent in writing of Malthouse Press Limited.

This book is sold subject to the condition that it shall not by way of trade, or otherwise, be lent, re-sold, hired out, or otherwise circulated without the publisher's prior consent in writing, in any form of binding or cover other than in which it is published and without a similar condition, including this condition, being imposed on the subsequent purchaser.

© Tanure Ojaide & Rose Aziza 2007
First Published 2007
ISBN 978 023 229 X

Distributors:
African Books Collective Ltd
Email: abc@africanbookscollective.com
Website: http://www.africanbookscollective.com

Acknowledgements

This project has been encouraged by the Office of the Vice Chancellor of Delta State University that also provided some funds for its publication.

Preface

This is a pioneering work in Urhobo Studies and meant to generate interest in the new discipline, which has recently been introduced to the curriculum of Delta State University. While Urhobo had been earlier studied at elementary and secondary school levels, the Urhobo Studies programme is the first of its kind in any university. The establishment of the programme has elevated the Urhobo language from the status of a language of only speech and daily conversation to that of an academic language being used for intellectual discourse. This, we believe, will make the language to further develop and more written than at any time before now. A language gains permanence through writing and studying, and writing Urhobo in the university will reduce the chances of its demise and not suffer the fate of many small languages that UNESCO forecasts will die off in a short time.

It is true, as stated in the first essay, that many individuals and associations have made efforts to have Urhobo written and studied in the past. However, the academy has its special way of conferring authority on a language taught by instructors to students with all the pedagogical and instructional facilities that a language laboratory and formal classroom gadgets and courses promote. Urhobo has rather belatedly entered the Nigerian academy, which up till recently, has been dominated by the majority languages of Hausa, Igbo, and Yoruba. Edo (that is, Bini) has for over a decade too been studied at the University of Benin.

It is significant that the Urhobo Studies programme at Delta State University has from the beginning been conceived to encompass more than the Urhobo language to include Urhobo civilization, culture, geography, history, and others. Urhobo Studies involve the totality of the people's experience. This work is the first and focuses on the language.

As will be seen from the essays, the language is studied from different perspectives. Working from the premise that language is the most significant cultural symbol of a people's identity, the writers show concern about the state of the language "today"; hence more than two essays discussing the challenges of the language in a post-modern, post-colonial, and global setting. Since culture is dynamic and language evolves with the people's changing experience, the book aptly starts with the evolution of the Urhobo language. Several writers see the threat and challenges posed by modernity and urbanisation to the culture with the language.

There are technical aspects of the language addressed by linguists, as the essays on tone, sound, lexis and structure, and code-mixing indicate. In a few cases, diagrams are provided to explain aspects of the language. Since language is not the restricted domain of only scholars of linguistics, other aspects of the language or issues that impinge on language use are also discussed. Since literature is a vehicle of language, the proverbs and axioms of the language as well as the oratorical and performance traditions in Urhobo are also discussed. Other cultural aspects, especially music, are also seen as enhancers of the language. To underscore the significance of religion and language, several writers examine the relationship between the Urhobo language and Christian evangelisation and between the language and the people's belief systems. A writer also explores the place of language in what has come to be known as Urhobo "disco" music.

The essays in the book reinforce each other; hence some points appear repeated. The closeness of several topics is meant to exhaustively open up the Urhobo language debate. Despite the closeness of a few topics, especially of the challenges of the language and culture and on evangelisation in Urhobo as well as Gospel music in Urhobo, each essay adds immensely to the overall issue of Urhobo language "today."

We hope that this pioneering group effort will be followed by individual and other group projects that will make the Urhobo language take its place in the register of modern African languages.

Tanure Ojaide
Rose Aziza

Contributors

Karo Ativie (MA) is a lecturer in the Department of English and Literary Studies, Delta State University, Abraka, Nigeria.

Sunny Awhefeada (MA) is a lecturer in the Department of English and Literary Studies, Delta State University, Abraka, Nigeria. He is working on a doctorate degree at the University of Ibadan, Nigeria.

Rose Aziza (PhD) is Head of Department of Languages and Linguistics and Director of the Urhobo Studies Programme at Delta State University, Abraka. Her doctoral dissertation was on the Urhobo language.

Godini G. Darah (PhD) is Professor and past Head of Department of English and Literary Studies, Delta State University, Abraka. A seasoned scholar and journalist, he is currently a Special Adviser on Communication to the Delta State Governor.

V.T. Jike (PhD) is the Director of the General Studies Unit and is a lecturer in the Department of Sociology, Delta State University, Abraka, Nigeria.

Macaulay Mowarin (MA) is a lecturer in the Department of English and Literary Studies, Delta State University, Abraka, Nigeria. He is working on a doctorate degree at the University of Ibadan, Nigeria.

S.O. Ogege teaches at Delta State University, Abraka.

Tanure Ojaide (PhD) is Professor of African-American and African Studies at the University of North Carolina at Charlotte. A scholar and writer, he has won many international prizes for his poetry.

Wilfred Onoriose (PhD) is Head of the Department of English and Literary Studies, Delta State University, Abraka, Nigeria.

Igho John Onose (PhD) is a lecturer in the Department of English and Literary Studies, Delta State University, Abraka. He once headed the Department.

Contents

Acknowledgements   *v*
Preface   *vi*

1. Evolution of the Urhobo language – *Tanure Ojaide*   1
2. The functions of tone in Urhobo and the need for tone-markers in the writing system – *Rose Aziza*   21
3. Lexis and structure in Urhobo – *Igho J. Onose*   33
4. Code-mixing: an investigation of English and Urhobo – *Karo Ative*   55
5. An overview of the sound system of Urhobo – *Rose Aziza*   63
6. The Urhobo language and the challenges of modernity – *Igho J. Onose*   83
7. Urhobo kingdoms and dialects – *W. Onoriose*   95
8. Urhobo culture and the challenges of modernisation – *G.G. Darah*   105
9. Urhobo proverbs and axioms – *Tanure Ojaide*   113
10. Linguistic correlates of 'salvation' in Urhobo religious cosmogony – *D.V. Jike* and *S. O. Ogege*   119
11. Urhobo gospel music – *M. Mowarin*   127
12. Praxis and aesthetics of Urhobo "disco" music – *Sunny Awhefeada*   133
13. The Urhobo orator – *Tanure Ojaide*   139
14. Teaching the word across languages: the Christian gospel in Urhobo – *Sunny Awhefeada*   151

Index   *155*

1

Evolution of the Urhobo language

- Tanure Ojaide

Introduction

Since the inception of modernity when writing spread over Africa with colonization, not much attention has been paid to the study of the Urhobo language. In other words, compared to, for instance, Hausa and Yoruba, native Urhobo speakers and outsiders have expressed little interest in the Urhobo language. If they had, much written or documented materials would be available today. It is much easier to document the evolution of a written language than a language such as Urhobo, which has basically, up till now, remained mainly oral/spoken. For decades in colonial and post-independence times in Nigeria, there has been neither strong cultural, religious, or political motivation, as in Hausa and Yoruba, to generate serious study of Urhobo.

Attention, though, has been paid to the language by especially the early missionaries in the land to facilitate converting the people into Christianity. The early interest was, thus, more of a missionary strategy to spread the gospel than an academic or cultural nationalist interest. Old Urhobo pastors, like Agori Iwe, and headmasters, like Francis Agboro and Daniel Obiomah, took interest in the language, but without a strong academic base in a university could not do much to develop the language. This is different from the Yoruba example in which educated missionaries were Yoruba who helped to write their own language. In Hausa, political motivation in colonial times, almost an imperial impulse in Northern Nigeria, galvanized interest in written Hausa. With the experience of written Arabic, writing Hausa in Roman letters became easy. Thus, political and religious factors accelerated the development of Hausa, factors that did not carry much resonance in Urhoboland. The Urhobo language needs a road map to chart its development from the beginning to the present. This will assist its current scholars to use the knowledge gained to revitalize the language through creative and academic writings as schools and universities teach it to young people overwhelmed by technological distractions of urban centres.

In the 1950s, 1960s, and early 1970s, Urhobo was used to teach children in the first three years or so of elementary school. This is understandable because English was then a new language that had to be taught through the native tongue to children. However, English was used as the language of learning from the fourth year of schooling. During those decades the Midwest (later Bendel) State Government commissioned the writing of books in Urhobo. Macmillan published a series of *Yon'Urhobo* by S.S. Ugheteni. The writer co-wrote the third volume with him. A lull followed this period for decades and Urhobo was not used to teach nor was it taught in schools in Urhoboland.

However, in recent times, there has been renewed interest in the Urhobo language. Scholars of Urhobo origin and social clubs with Urhobo nationalist ideals have mainly generated this interest. These scholars include Peter Ekeh, G.G. Darah, and Rose Aziza. Urhobo Social Club, with branches in cities outside Urhobo all over Nigeria, has also promoted the speaking and writing of Urhobo language. In the 1980s, the Club was very active in bringing Urhobo elites together to promote the culture and language. The study of Urhobo language is seen as an integral element of Urhobo Studies, which include culture, society, history, literature, music, and art. Works of Darah and the writer on *Udje* dance songs and Rose Aziza's doctoral dissertation and academic essays on Urhobo tone system have all focused on and clarified aspects of the Urhobo language. In addition, contributions by others in a journal such as *Studies in Art, Religion & Culture Among the Urhobo and Isoko People* and Perkins Foss's study of Urhobo arts have also advanced some aspects of the language.

This study, therefore, attempts to integrate aspects of earlier studies and go further to focus on the evolution of the Urhobo language from the beginning to now. As a result of modernization and urbanization, the language is losing fluent native speakers. In other words, of the Urhobo people, especially educated and urbanized, who identify themselves as Urhobo, only a fraction can speak the language fluently. The study of the evolution of the language, therefore, is an attempt to know where we *are* and what needs to be done to arrest the demise of the language and the knowledge and civilization that it carries.

A people's language is their greatest cultural means of identity. Its evolution corresponds with the evolution of its people. Culture is dynamic, and so is language. The Urhobo language has continued to evolve from its early speakers to the present (the beginning of the twenty-first century). It suffices to state again that it is more difficult to chart the evolution of an oral language than a written one. From the permanent and reliable archive of written or literary materials, one can easily glean changes in vocabulary, grammar, idioms, and other aspects of a language. This study relies on theory of language evolution, interviews with old and knowledgeable Urhobo speakers like Chiefs Dozen

Ogbariemu of Iwhrekan and Dickson Onojegbe of Ughelli, study of folklore, and scanty written materials. Ask the ordinary Urhobo person in the street in the town or village what words such as *babotu*, *iduru*, and *erugbe* mean, and they would stare at you as if you were speaking a strange language. Chief Dozen Ogbariemu told me that many contemporary Urhobo people are so ignorant of ancient Urhobo that a mother named her daughter "Babotu." If the mother knew that *babotu* meant prostitute, she would have given a more courteous name to her daughter! If the trend is not arrested in the towns, Urhobo could go the way of many small languages that UNESCO predicts would gradually die off. This study is part of a concerted effort to reverse the negative course for the flourishing of a language that carries so much poetry, philosophy, and knowledge that need to guide its indigenes in particular and others in general to better cope with the vagaries of life and modern problems. To go further, one has to know how things have been from the past to the present to know what direction to take.

A language's evolution is directly affected by its speakers'/people's origin, environment, history, neighbours, and internal and external dynamics that involve society, economy, and politics. These factors continue to shape and reshape it. Over time, language inevitably sheds some of its words, expressions, and grammar even as it appropriates new ones. Language, therefore, continuously discards and absorbs words in an internal logic that ensures vitality in its growth. Urhobo has particularly gone this course, and the study of its evolution is illuminated by these factors. The primeval origin, waves of migration and absorption of vocabulary during the odyssey, colonialism, modernism with its capitalism and industrialization, urbanization, and the living reality all have strong imprints on the language.

Urhobo is both the language and the people who speak it. Though the population of those who identify themselves as Urhobo is currently about three million, the speakers of the language are not as many. Many of those who live in the urban centres of Effurun, Sapele, Ughelli, and Warri do not speak the language, but speak more of Pidgin English. Most of the Urhobo under twenty-one and living in cities have been so urbanized and modernized that they understand little and almost do not speak their mother tongue.

The Urhobo language

Urhobo belongs to the Niger-Congo family of West African languages. The Pan-Africanist scholar of African cultures and their achievements, Cheikh Anta Diop, has observed similarities among black African languages very far apart from their loci. This large "family" to which Urhobo belongs lends credence to the Great Bantu Migration idea or theory of a common source of most sub-

Saharan African languages. Chief Ogbariemu told me that the Urhobo people had their distant origin in Egypt, from where they moved through Borno to Ife and then to "Aka," Benin. Despite the Babel that later ensued, a "family" has many branches of the same tree! Urhobo is said to belong to the Niger-Kordofan group of the language family. Jocelyn Murray's "family" traits appear in the tonal Urhobo.

On a narrower and more specific level, Urhobo belongs to the Pan-Edo group of languages deriving from the eponymous "Aka," what Kay Williamson and other Niger Delta language scholars describe as *Edoid*. Legends and other extant folklore sources indicate that some ten and more centuries ago, ethnic groups, which are now autonomous, once shared a common space (Aka) from where they migrated at different times in history for different reasons. The Urhobo, in different waves, especially because of the tyranny of the Ogisos and the pressure for land, moved southwards into their present homeland. According to Onigu Otite, there were two waves of migration: the common people and the nobility. The migration establishes the enduring relationship between Urhobo and other Edoid and neighbouring languages. The different groups that migrated at different times during the Ogiso Dynasty may also be responsible for the many variants and different dialects of Urhobo.

There is ample linguistic evidence that Urhobo is related to Bini, Ishan (Esan), and Ora that make up the Pan-Edo or Edoid group. Urhobo is also remotely related to some other Nigerian languages such as Igala and Yoruba and to the Ghanaian Ewe and Fanti. Many words in Urhobo and Bini are the same, as in Ishan and Ora. The attentive Urhobo speaker can almost follow a discussion in Ishan, as many of its words and their pronunciations are the same. Words for "water," "money," "come," and so many others are the same. A binding legend in the folklore of the Edoid groups is that of Ogiso ("*ogie iso*"/king of the sky). Even the writer's own Urhobo name of Ojaide appears to be a bastardization of Bini for "removed from suffering". The name also appears related to the Ishan "*ogie ide*" (the king never falls) and also to the Yoruba Jakande. The Yoruba connection as of Old Oyo links Urhobo and Ewe whose folklore has Agokoli a tyrant similar to Ogiso. Many names in Igala and Idoma sound familiar in Urhobo. An Ujevwe name like Ubiogba has resonance in Igala, and "*ogba*" though pronounced differently means fence in both Urhobo and Igala. Also in the Igala language, the word for drive is the same as the Urhobo *gua*. Thus, Igala's "*Agw' imoto*" (we are driving a car) is the same as the Urhobo "*Avware gu' imoto*." Different spelling methods of the consonant cluster *gwa* and *gua* are really the same. Also a word like "*oji*" in both languages means thief.

Many Urhobo and Yoruba words are the same and, while nobody can ascertain who borrowed from whom, there is the probability of common sources and interactions. Urhobo people have for long migrated to Bini and Yoruba "bushes" to pursue their palm oil producing work. Some Urhobo use *ogun* for iron; no doubt related to the popular Yoruba god. Also in an Owhawha song, there is mention of "*ajakpa*," which is the Yoruba for the tortoise. Some known words of Yoruba origin have been domesticated. For instance, the Yoruba "*akara*" for fried bean cake is in Urhobo either the same "*akara*" or "*ikara*." Other neighbours such as the Ijo, Itsekiri, and Ukwani (Igbo) have also loaned words to Urhobo. The aim of this demonstration of Urhobo's closeness to other languages is to establish its origin and nature to better detail its evolution.

The Urhobo live in twenty-two polities called clans during the British colonial administration and now generally referred to as kingdoms. Each of the polity has its own variant, rather dialect, of Urhobo. While the Agbarho variant of Urhobo is generally accepted as Standard Urhobo, the language has many dialects, most of which are mutually intelligible. Up to the early 1960s, Isoko was part of Urhobo but made a political decision to separate and assert its autonomy as a people and language. Generally, Agbarho, Agbon, and Ughelli, barely distinguishable, seem to be the common Urhobo. Ujevwe and Udu are variants that are very musical but carry many differences from Standard Urhobo. However, Okpe and Uvwie (Evwron) are more out of line from the common Urhobo. The Okpe tend to claim a more direct affinity to Benin than the other Urhobo groups. In fact, at some times in the past, the Okpe have claimed that they were not Urhobo. It is ironical that Isoko is more comprehensible than the Urhobo dialects of Okpe and Uvwie. The diversity of variants of the Urhobo language is important in the evolution of the language into a more uniform tongue.

Urhobo neighbours

The Urhobo people's neighbours have contributed to the evolution of the Urhobo language, which has developed over centuries, into what it is today. As already explained of the *Edoid* groups, Urhobo vocabulary is replete with retained words from the common ancestral Aka and the residence at Udo that saw many groups migrate into different directions in today's Delta and Edo States of Nigeria. Numerical words and the counting system in particular are very similar in Ishan, Ora, and Urhobo.

Other Urhobo neighbours are the Ukwani (Igbo), Ijo, and Itsekiri. The Urhobo people came from the eponymous Aka in two main routes: by water via the River Niger and its creeks and by land across the Ethiope River, some claim in the present Abraka area. Those that came by land make up the northern Urhobo groups such as Abraka, Agbon, and Okpe and retain much of the Bini language. It is significant that there is another Okpe in Edo State and "Agbon" in Bini means home, no doubt a sigh of relief after settling permanently after decades of migration. Urhobo today does not call home *"agbon"* as in Bini but *"uwevwin."*

The group that came by water passed the Ukwuani area and first settled in current Ijo territory of Ugobri in current Bayelsa State. The group of Urhobo migrants that came through Igbo territory along the Niger and its creeks absorbed some of their words. This early interaction and the subsequent close neighbourliness resulted in the limited linguistic commonality between Urhobo and the Ukwani dialect of Igbo. Words such as *enu* (sky), *ọgọ* (in-law), *ofigbo* (palm-oil), *ọpia* (cutlass), and *ugagbe* (mirror/glass), among others, illustrate the limited shared vocabulary. Okoro, a common Igbo name today, seems to derive from Bini and has an Urhobo variant in Okorho. It is significant that Orogun and its satellite towns and villages such as Aragba and Emonu bordering on the Ukwani speak and understand both Urhobo and Ukwani (Igbo) fluently. Similarly, the Ukwani border communities of Obiaruku and Abi understand and speak some Urhobo. Urhobo and Ukwani people, especially in border areas, go to each other's markets and have inter-married considerably to establish a relationship that their individual languages have helped to cement. This must have been the same for other Urhobo neighbours such as the Ijo and the Itsekiri.

In addition to markets and inter-marriages, other factors have affected Urhobo loan words from Ijo and Itsekiri. Masquerade cults of water spirits of the Ijo affect southern Urhobo people who live in a similar terrain. At masquerade performances all over Urhobo, most of the songs are in Ijo or Urhobo laced with Ijo expressions. It is mainly in the area of names that the Urhobo people appropriated Ijo. The town of Oginibo in the Ujevwe part of Ughelli North Local Government is an Ijo expression, *Igoni bo* (It's strangers that have arrived!) Many Urhobo neighbours of Ijo give Ijo names to their children. Examples are Opuama, Tobi, and Pela, all of which became great families in Urhoboland.

Many southern Urhobo people call the sea goddess *Umalokun* and the sea as *oku*, the same as in Itsekiri. The Itsekiri, particularly in trade with Europeans before and after the inception of colonialism, were middlemen who went between the Urhobo and the Europeans. This was so during the Slave Trade and the palm-oil trade that continued till the middle of the twentieth century. These commercial interactions often had their social manifestations. Many Urhobo and Itsekiri are also bound in intermarriages. There is barely an Itsekiri without some Urhobo blood or relations, as any Urhobo without some close or distant Itsekiri connection. Before the current problems between the two groups in Warri because of land, the Itsekiri went inland to set up communities in Urhoboland as in Ohrerhe in Agbarho and Otumara in Agbon. Sometimes the Itsekiri give names to Urhobo towns as Obodo for Orhuwherun. This process of interaction definitely impacted on language borrowing on both sides. Many Urhobo people use some Itsekiri words even in cases where indigenous Urhobo words are also available. Many Urhobo also call head-tie *ulẹso*, umbrella *achicha*, and sea *oku*. As a result of the popularization of *Amebo* in the 'Village Headmaster' television programme, there was a debate on the etymology of the name. While the Urhobo claim it is a bastardization of *Avwebọ* (favourite wife/darling), the Itsekiri say it is their word and name. The Urhobo words for child (*ọmọ*) and wife (*aye*) resonate meaningfully in Itsekiri and Yoruba ears.

While there has also been close interaction among the Urhobo and the Ijo, this has not resulted in as much language influence as the Itsekiri relationship. As earlier said, the masquerade cult has influenced Urhobo with its rituals. In Urhobo border towns, as Okwagbe with large markets, there is no doubt that language borrowings are common for effective trade transactions.

Ancient Urhobo

The original Urhobo must be lost in history, as its orality has not been effectively carried forward by memory alone. Memory tends to fade after a long time and what is passed by only word of mouth and so not documented in writing can get lost. This poses a threat to the historiography of the Urhobo people and also to a reliable road map from the past to the present, as far as the language is concerned. While there was the early missionary interest in writing and teaching Urhobo, the gains of the 1940s, 1950s, and early 1960s were arrested in the ethnic rivalry of Midwest and later Bendel State. The failure to agree on what three or so languages out of over a dozen of the State to adopt in radio and television news resulted in the use of English and Pidgin English for news rather than indigenous languages like Bini and Urhobo.

The oldest form of Urhobo appears to be mainly esoteric today. All Urhobo elders unanimously agree that much of Urhobo derived from Bini. According to Chief Dozen Ogbariemu, this fact is not disputed. Now 84, when he was young he heard his own grandfather speak Urhobo that was closer to Bini. In fact, according to him, Urhobo foreparents understood Bini. With the interaction with different neighbours and groups, the specificity of a new environment, and the process of time, Bini gradually wore out to the Urhobo spoken today.

The ancient Urhobo language seems to be limited today to *epha* (divination) and traditional religions and medicines. This is apparently close to Bini (Aka) as divination begins with the invocation of Ominigbo, the executed Benin diviner who foretold the destruction of Benin by the British, which resulted in the slaughter of 1897. It is interesting, as Sam Erivwo observes, that the Urhobo for divination, *epha*, has obvious generic origin with the Yoruba *Ifa*, the Igbo *Afa*, the Edo *Iha*, Akoko Edo *Ivha*, the Isoko *Eva*, and the Nupe *Eba*. Kofi Awoonor also sees this relationship with the Ewe *Afa*. The naming of divination strings in Urhobo such as Okanra, Obara, Ogbi, Ophu, One, and Oghori and others as Erhokpe, Eka, Erhure, Ete, Orhan, Ighite, and Ogbi derive from the ancient

Urhobo language of primordial times when humans could hold dialogue with God, gods, and spirits. Also of this ancient Urhobo are the paraphernalia of divination. The diviner uses the tooth of a warthog to strike the seeds of the *agbragha* tree. The ensuing language is ancient. Examples are: "*Aba ru ghute*," "*Obi na vwara*," and "*Odi na be*." The last expression means that danger is at hand.

Similarly, the Urhobo of festivals and medicinal and other rituals reflects Urhobo that is millennia old. In different parts of Urhobo, at festival times, the invocations and prayers for the exorcising of evil from the communities are done in an arcane Urhobo. Traditional healers also use many terms, not contemporary, to convey meaning to impress their wishes on the patients. It is revealing to note that at the burial ceremony of an adult, the ritual performers say "*Uhri kpa ikebe me rio oghwa*." This is very meaningful Bini for a proverbial saying that the *uhri* tree being cut should fall down so that its cutter can go back home. It is meant to solicit the gods or ancestors to open *Urhoro* gates for the deceased to be fully integrated into the ancestral realm.

Two other sources of ancient Urhobo are cultural practices such as body marks and folklore. Very old men and women have body marks that are special to Urhobo people. In ancient times these body marks were used for clan and ethnic identity. With such, the Urhobo knew their own people and did not take them as captives into servitude or hurt them. Such marks as shown in Onigu Otite's *Urhobo People* include "*akprusi*," and attest to a language whose original vocabulary and tenor have changed drastically over centuries.

In many Urhobo folktales, there are songs. Many of such songs do not have any semantic meaning as far as contemporary Urhobo is concerned. It is easy for folklorists and scholars to dismiss such songs as meaningless verbal sorties meant to entertain, but it is likely that at some time deep in the past, they made meaning among the singers of tales and their audiences. Also one kind of Urhobo riddles appears to relate to a language that made meaning at its beginning but no longer so. When the riddle spinner says: "*Kukuruku beberebe!*" the response is that the pepper plant's seeds fall beside it. Doubtless, the phrasing is onomatopoeic and musical, but many ancient words appear to have been formed with those sound effects in mind.

The Urhobo environment

The Urhobo environment, in its physical manifestations of land, rivers, fauna and flora, and spirituality as shown in belief systems, has contributed not only to the typicality of the language but also to its evolution. Wherever groups of Urhobo came from at different historical periods to meet others in their present homeland became subsumed in the reality of the place. A people's culture results from the way they adapt to the "nature" around them. The Urhobo people are no exception to this cultural theory. Once the people got settled, the quest for relevance became a concern for them, as they started to "name" what is with and around them. Language expands with the broadening knowledge and experience of its speakers.

The Urhobo terrain can be divided into southern and northern sections. As described elsewhere:

> The southern Urhobo have as neighbours the Isoko to the southeast, the Itsekiri to the west, and the Ijo to the south. They live across mangrove swamps and very luxuriant rain forests. The major occupations of these groups of Urhobo are fishing, hunting, and farming. Those to their north, far from the wide rivers but still riverine, also farm, hunt, and fish. These northern Urhobo have the Bini to the north and the Ukwani (Igbo) to the northeast. Interspersed with thick luxuriant evergreen forests, oil-palm trees abound here and provide the source of palm-oil produce at which the Urhobo are especially skilled (Otite 10). Rubber trees started to be planted after WWI, making rubber collection a major occupation of many in the rural areas. The two main seasons are the wet and dry periods. The wet/rainy season (April to October) has a short dry spell called August Break. In the dry season, there is the cold period called Harmattan (*owhawha*), which spans from December to early February. Nowadays, many Urhobo live in urban areas. The urban Urhobo are mainly traders (Ojaide).

In the formation and evolution of Urhobo language, the environment is important because it is the nature to which humans respond, and which results in the people's culture, experience, and reality. Of course, language is the most powerful vehicle of culture. The spatial locus of the Urhobo people gives rise to experiences, which demand articulation in spoken form and so nurture the language. Geography and history are major forces in a people's culture. If the environment undergoes changes, as Urhobo has done for decades, especially with colonialism and oil prospecting, the language correspondingly changes.

The Urhobo environment is not only physical but also spiritual. Many of the physical things assume spiritual symbolism as the *oghriki* planted in new settlements at town centres. The *uloho*, iroko, became a godlike figure for prosperity. In the Orogun area, the monitor, *ogborigbo*, assumed totemic significance. The point being made here is that it is the environment of traditional people that gives rise to their spiritual and religious pursuits. The immediate and familiar become part of daily realities that language has to contend with. Hence the world-view, sensibility, and beliefs of a people are integral parts of the environment. Urhobo myths, mainly etiological, explain the natural phenomena around to make it comprehensible to those who live in the area.

Urhobo religions are significant vehicles of the language and as the religions change or evolve, so also does the language. As noted of the early Urhobo Christian missionaries, the current upsurge of Pentecostal churches all over Urhoboland will influence the language. The few pastors that evangelize in Urhobo have to creatively invent new coinages in the language to convey the ideas and concerns of the new faith. Urhobo language, thus, continues to evolve according to the manner the environment impacts upon the lives of the people.

Urhobo history and European encounter

In addition to the environment and geography, the leading factor that has driven the evolution of the Urhobo language is history. The society which, as a result of foreign interactions, changes from traditionalism to modernity is bound to affect the language. Traditional society tends to admit few changes and does so grudgingly. The rites, rituals, and other ceremonies that give stability and continuity to the people's way of life remain about the same for as long as the people can keep them. However, change can be inevitable when more powerful external agents are responsible. This was the case in parts of traditional Africa as Urhoboland that European powers colonized from the later part of the nineteenth century to the middle of the twentieth. European incursion into Africa for the purpose of commerce and colonization and "modern" government in post-independent Nigeria all have bearing on the evolution of the Urhobo language. A language develops by absorbing new vocabulary relevant to its speakers and simultaneously discarding in a slow process what is no longer relevant or outmoded. The Urhobo language goes through this process in its evolution.

The first Europeans that apparently reached Urhoboland were the Portuguese. A certain Pereira, a Portuguese explorer, was said to have observed in 1505 that "in the hinterland beyond the Forcados River, lived the Sobou or Sobo, a name that was corrected to Urhobo in 1938 (Otite). This early contact would leave lasting impressions on the Urhobo people, who called the Portuguese "Potokri." Urhobo elders thought these white people were their ancestors come back to life because of their ghostly "white" pink colour. Coming from the sea in ships, which brought luxury goods and new ideas and religion (Christianity), the Urhobo people received them with what they brought. This is the long association of the sea and its goddess with wealth and the Urhobo saying *"Olokun bie emu rhe vwe"* (Olokun, bring wealth to me).

Since many European cultures have a common origin, many Portuguese words absorbed into the Urhobo lexicon also have Spanish and French connotations. The following Urhobo words are neologisms that derive from the

Portuguese: *oro* (gold), *ukujęrę* (spoon), *ǫsete* (plate), *imęję* (table), *sabato* (shoes), *ughǫjǫ* (watch/clock), and perhaps *isama* (salmon or canned fish). As luxury articles that the Europeans bartered for Urhobo produce, especially palm oil, they easily got into the vocabulary of Urhobo daily speech. Urhobo language is a dynamic cultural vehicle that carries along new coinages to better express and communicate new experiences in an ever-changing world.

The greatest European impact on Urhobo though is the British colonization of Nigeria. Colonialism is an economic enterprise of the militarily strong at the expense of the weak. The so many ethnic nationalities that occupy what comprises contemporary Nigeria were not united and armed to ward off British imperialism. Britain took over Nigeria with force of arms and entered the Urhobo area in the 1910s. Colonialism introduced new dimensions to the lives of the people. It brought capitalism, which shifted emphasis on ethical and moral values to monetary power. To the Urhobo, *idǫlǫ* (dollar/money), rather than happiness, became the main object of pursuit in life. The British imposed a poll tax (*osa uyovwin*) on every male adult. At a time (about the 1930s), the tax was seven shillings, which took the hard worker all the palm oil produce of a season! It is worth noting that the Urhobo people saw taxation as a "head fee," because without paying it, one was arrested and jailed—so you have to save your head by paying the white man's "debt."

The British colonial government established councils, districts, and divisions. Ughelli became the headquarters of Urhobo Division. Police, army, departments (later ministries), sanitary inspectors, forest guards, and schools, among others, came to be parts of the Urhobo people's society. Churches were almost always related to schools. These indices of colonialism were seen as agents of modernity. The new experiences have a profound impact on the Urhobo language.

Urhobo has absorbed, found new words (neologisms), or Urhoboized English words, which came out of this contact that has remained a major historical experience of the people. Urhobo joins many words, as in the German language, to form new words by stringing already existing words. A good example of a German word of this category is "krakenhaus" (literally house of the sick) for hospital. Urhobo calls airplane *okǫ-enu* (sky canoe) and car *okǫ-oto* (land canoe). With rivers, streams, and creeks in abundance in the rainforest area, the people have always had canoes and rafts that became the source for the naming of the modern car and airplane. Thus, while some words deriving from the postcolonial experience have a straight Urhobo name as of *idjighere* for bicycle and *okuna* (which appears to be a compression of *okǫ r'ona*/canoe that flares light) for ship, most other borrowings are localized. Examples include *igǫmeti* (government) *ipolisi* (police), *imoto* (motor car), *arupleni* (airplane), *igramafonu* (gramophone), *itelevishǫni* (television), *irhedio* (radio), and *ividio* (video). An Urhobo word like *ipoko* (pork) seems to have fully been subsumed into Urhobo because of its early arrival with the Europeans. In fact, there is an important Okwagbe family called Ipoko!

The foreign words in Urhobo which are either localized or Urhoboized, all in their new Urhobo renditions start with one of the language's vowels: a, e, e, i, o, o, u. The predominance of such words beginning with *i* can thus be understood. While, generally, the dialects of Udu and Ujevwe do without the vowels and start words, especially names, with consonants, the Standard Urhobo tends to start every word with a vowel.

A language whose speakers do not have a modern technological base, Urhobo has not fared well in new technological terms. While French may have its Academie Francaise, and some African languages like Hausa and Yoruba have organizations that "standardize" the language, Urhobo up to now has none of such regulatory bodies. Urhobo, thus, evolves erratically, absorbing English and novel post-modern and technological terms by either concatenating verbal translations or using the native accent to domesticate the foreign words and terms.

Urhobo has not absorbed modern terms effortlessly. However, the challenge has remained in non-material, spiritual, and intellectual terms from modern scholarship. Sometimes Urhobo is sucked into the binary world of the Europeans as it attempts to "name" new experiences derived from foreign religions. The Urhobo *ofuafo* can be "white," "clean," or "holy" in English. The Urhobo *obiebi* can mean dark, black, green, and more. These terms assumed importance in Christian parlance of the dichotomy between the good and the bad. The limitation of Urhobo to absorb shades of colours and other subtleties that express European or modern terms is a big challenge to Urhobo language scholars. Urhobo colours are limited and the language seems inadequate to communicate shades of colours. Even in counting, it takes an adept to count to a million! It is recently that Edward Osubele invented *ima ovo* for one trillion.

Missionary language projects in Urhobo

At this juncture, I want to recount the effort made by Urhobo-born missionaries to initially promote the language. Their effort sometimes coalesces with that of teachers in the new colonial schools. While they were interested in propagating their brands of Christianity, one should pay tribute to the efforts of the pioneers of Urhobo language study. According to G. G. Darah, in the 1920s T. Emedo and W.A. Tadaferue pioneered the Urhobo translation of the Scriptures. A primer of Okpe dialect was published in 1921 by Ofodidun, an Urhobo who had done evangelical work among Urhobo migrant workers in the Ikale district of Ondo Province. A major motivation of the translations into Urhobo in church and school circles was nationalistic as the Urhobo Christians in Sapele, Warri,

Eku, and Ughelli struggled to free themselves from the imposition of Yoruba on them by the Anglican Church. At a time, the church insisted that Urhobo converts had to read catechisms and take baptismal tests in Yoruba. The ensuing revolt against this practice led to the founding of new churches as the Baptist Mission by Aganbi at Eku (Darah). In addition to the catechism, hymn and prayer books started to be in Urhobo from these missionary efforts.

Darah continues that "By the 1950s, school administrators like Ahwinahwin of Ughelli and B. Onokpasa of Okpe did translations of Urhobo oral literature. The complete Urhobo Bible was available in the 1960s and since the 1970s Canon Oghenekaro's Urhobo Language Committee has been working on improved language primers and readers." These are preliminary efforts that did not go far enough but at least pointed to a direction that could greatly advance the Urhobo language.

Internal poetic dynamics

There have also been internal Urhobo indigenous practices that have enhanced the creativity of the language. A major artistic phenomenon of pre-colonial and colonial times was the practice of *Udje* dance songs. It is significant that the process of composing songs was a very poetic and creative one. The sophistication of the Urhobo language today partly derives from the performance of *Udje* dance songs, which at a time spread all over Urhobo. In its heydays from about 1850 to the 1940s, almost every group in Urhobo was involved in *Udje* dance song performance. Since the master artists were from Ujevwe and Udu, these were hired to Uvwię, Agbon, and elsewhere to teach these people this performance tradition. Oloya and Memerume, the acclaimed masters of the artistic tradition of Iwhrekan and Edjophe respectively, travelled wide in Urhobo to propagate their songs. The rest of Urhobo should have absorbed the singing tongue of the Ujevwe and Udu, and helped to fashion Urhobo into what it is today. This is a major internal cultural factor that drives the dynamism of the language.

Urhobo national character

The Urhobo language has evolved according to the history and national character of the people. The historical side has been dealt with. The Urhobo people have evolved from different groups and clans into a nation with a specific identity. The efforts of Mukoro Mowoe in this regard have been recognized. From personal observation and according to Otite, the Urhobo are very republican in character. There is aggressive individualism, reinforced by worship of Ivwri with the concept of strong leadership qualities. The Urhobo person has self-pride and often boasts of self-reliance. The saying, "Wọ ghẹ ro vwe?" (Do you feed me?) is a reflection of the individuality and self-pride. This individualism runs parallel to a sense of community inherited from ancient times in common ownership of ponds and farms and the *ifo* practice in which you help others in, for instance, roofing or clearing a farm and others in their turn helping you when you need them.

The Urhobo character has consistently affected the evolution of names (*ode*), praise names (*odova*), and proverbs (*ise*). The values of the people, their belief systems, and world-view are expressed in names. Names are very important aspects of a language and its culture and civilization. The emphasis on children, prosperity, and long life is reflected in names such as Omonefe, Owhonigho, Omonigho, and Irikefe. It is significant that Urhobo names continue to be popular and those who barely speak the language take pride in having Urhobo names, many of which are now short rather than the *ite* type used to send subliminal messages to ancestors, family, rivals, or foes. Names such as Udumebraye (They are afraid of me), Omotejowho (A girl is also a human being), Ochibejivwie (A eunuch has now got a child), and many others seem to be more ancient and confined now to rural areas. Most names of young people nowadays are simple or the shortened form of long names — Ese, Efe, Ufuoma, Ejiro, Tasa, Tega, etc. For instance, Tega is the shortened form of Oghenetega.

Since proverbs and axioms constitute the most creative side of language, some comment on Urhobo proverbs is necessary. The proverbs are ancient and seem to express a world-view of traditional times. The limited world of pre-colonial times has conditioned many Urhobo proverbs, which modernity and science in particular can contradict. But these expressions remain a repository of knowledge and wisdom.

Government communication/language policies

It is also significant that Urhobo language has flourished as a result of independent Nigerian policies on language and communication. Radio and television news, as done by Amraibure and Ukere, have brought Urhobo people to listen attentively to what is happening around them and beyond. First at Ibadan, then at Benin, and currently at both Warri and Asaba, Urhobo translations of news in English have many listeners. Television programmes in Urhobo or English spiced with Urhobo (as of Kokori in the Bendel State television programme, "Hotel de Jordan," in the 1970s) have been very successful in promoting the Urhobo language. Once a language gets to be written, it assumes the significance of permanence. One can now go into the archives of Radio Nigeria, Ibadan, or Benin, Warri, and Asaba and research into Urhobo written for reading. In other words, one can now see the difference between Urhobo meant for radio and television newscasters and other broadcast forms and the common Urhobo.

Modernity and urbanization

Urhobo is still evolving. A major effect of colonialism and modernity is increasing communication and access to one another. Formerly isolated Urhobo villages and clans have opened up as a result of a good network of roads. More than ever before, the Urhobo people are one close community. The mass movement to urban areas has also brought different Urhobo dialects together, and in the ensuing interaction, as with mixed marriages, a blending of tongues continues to reshape the language into a new form. This has resulted in more and more people of other polities speaking the "standard" Agbarho dialect of Urhobo. It is becoming increasingly common for the Uvwie and Okpe to speak the common Urhobo in public occasions. Similarly, in my research into *Udje* dance songs in Ewu, Olomu, Udu, and Ujevwe, the singers, knowing that I am of Agbon origin, spoke the general Urhobo to me for easy communication. While the different dialects remain particularly strong in rural areas, there is a growing acceptance of one Urhobo, the "standard" one. Many Okpe villages, especially border ones, speak the general Urhobo.

This coalescing of dialects and variants into a common usage in urban centres has its implication for the vocabulary and accent/intonation of Urhobo. Words that used to be special to some dialects, like Udu and Ujevwe, like *orose* and *alauke* for tortoise, have entered the common usage and are used as well as *ogbeyin*. Urbanization, office work, and trading are assisting to fuse the dialects into the mainstream. The Urhobo spoken by youths almost everywhere in Urhobo and in the urban settlements is changing. It is becoming more contracted and elliptical. For instance, the general Urhobo greeting of *"Mi guọ!"* is now just *"Iguọ!"* Also, for instance, normal prosodic arrangements are contracted. Older people still say *"Kpa iroro vrẹ"* (Forget about it.) Younger Urhobo speakers are likely to say *"Kpa iroro."* The palm-oil soup traditionally called *oghwevwri* is currently called just *oghwo*. It could be that the pressure and rush culture of the city demands a more concise language than the more leisurely one of traditional times.

There are enduring signs in the state of the Urhobo language that bring hope that the language will evolve into a stronger form in the near future. Certain socio-cultural and political happenings are helping in this direction. Many extended family, clan, and ethnic associations abound and they promote interaction in Urhobo. There are monthly meetings either on a chosen Saturday or Sunday on one of the weeks. Through such meetings, the older speakers of the language assist less proficient younger speakers to acquire better speaking skills.

The umbrella organization of the Urhobo People is the Urhobo Progressive Union (UPU), whose founding President was Mukoro Mowoe. In modern times, there are the Ufuoma and Eguono Clubs and others that bring same-minded people together. Some of the associations are for men, others for women; some mixed, and yet others for the youths and the so-called elites. There is, for example, the Okpara Elites Association. I have already mentioned Urhobo Social Club. There is in Lagos Atamu Social Club, whose membership is made up of enterprising Urhobo professionals. In these clubs and associations, Urhobo is the medium of communication. Many of them sponsor events and ceremonies, which promote the Urhobo language.

On social occasions, especially wedding/marriage ceremonies, burial events, and parties, Urhobo "orators" are hired to entertain. This is the modernization of the "Otota" of traditional times. The *ọtota* is the spokesperson of a family, village, or group. The individual is expected to have facility with words and know how to meander through intricacies of thought. *Ọtota* carries the responsibilities of modern diplomats and negotiators. Perhaps the best-known of the many "orators' in Urhobo today is Ofua. Others include Achanacho. Their facility with words, wit, and humour makes such occasions not only interesting but also reiterate the innate and creative resources of the language they are revitalizing and developing. Such social events bring people together in a community that listens and critiques the stretching of the language into new frontiers.

Urhobo musicians and poets, in their compositions, continue to reinvigorate the language. As noted earlier, studies by G.G. Darah and the writer of *Udje* dance songs show the poetic, musical, and dramatic richness of Urhobo. Omokomoko Osiokpa and the late Ogute Otan, in their various musical pieces, have tapped from the unlimited wealth of the language. Similarly, Sally Young has used Urhobo to sing many dance songs to which young and old respond enthusiastically. New musicians like Erhibo Okpa and Johnson Adjan, in playing Urhobo disco at public ceremonies, have drawn much attention to the vitality of the language. People pick up the songs and sing them at home and workplaces.

The establishment of Urhobo Studies at Delta State University, Abraka, is a major effort to popularize Urhobo with its folklore, history, and civilization. The Director of the Urhobo Studies Programme, Rose Aziza, is putting much energy and resources into the project, which is strongly supported by the institution's Vice Chancellor, Uvie Igun. The availability of a language laboratory, the invitation of guest speakers, reading of poems, workshops and seminars, and the regular teaching are all advancing the Urhobo language project. It is a challenge of the Urhobo Studies Programme to establish a modern orthography for the language. Up till now, there are different spellings reflecting various dialects.

The academicians may have to push for the acceptance of Urhobo orthography, which is haphazard at the moment. Writing the language has to move from dotting the *es* and *os* to indicate sounds of *er* and *or* respectively. Currently, Hausa and Yoruba have established orthographies and have moved to tap on new technologies by having fonts that reflect the sound modulations of the languages. Urhobo, as a tonal language, needs to integrate into the Kwa font or establish a font that is specific to the language as Macintosh computer programmes make available.

Recent academic progress

In recent years academic work has greatly moved Urhobo from an only spoken language to a written and intellectual language. In the 1980s, the *Eta Urhobo Magazine* was founded to push the frontiers of mass communication in Urhobo. Ukere of the University of Benin about 1990 brought out the first written Urhobo lexicon. The renowned artist, Bruce Onobrakpeya, has, in his forays into Urhobo folklore, invented an Urhobo sign language. In 1997, *Urhobo Voice* hit the streets. It is, no doubt, the most widely circulated Urhobo paper. Far away in North America, the Urhobo Historical Society through *WADOO* is projecting Urhobo language and experience. It has a web site: www.wadoo.com.

Also in recent years there has been the publication of an Urhobo dictionary. This shows the coming of age of Urhobo language evolution. Ayemenokpe Edward Osubele, who has taught at Federal Government College, Odogbolu, for a long time, pioneered the dictionary project. *A Dictionary of Urhobo Language* is a monumental work that rekindles interest in the language. The dictionary has two sections: one of Urhobo words and their translations in English and the other words in English with their Urhobo translations. The work makes it easy for both native speakers and learners of the language to look for words. Osubele is the Dr. Samuel Johnson of Urhobo, and one expects expanded editions of the first imprint at regular intervals.

The strength of a language goes beyond the spoken and the written words. After all, words are signs for communication. The language is a vehicle of a people's values and civilization and the development of Urhobo language should proceed *pari pasu* with the study of Urhobo history, culture, the arts, and others. A language's strength too is not only based on the number of its speakers but also more on its development to carry intellectual and complex thought. Yoruba has been able to achieve this, a feat the Igbo language has not been able to match. Urhobo can be strong from the intellectual input of its speakers and scholars.

Pidgin English and Urhobo

One cannot ignore the impact of Pidgin English on Urhobo and vice versa. As a result of the urbanization, most Urhobo in towns like Effurun, Warri, and Sapele speak both Urhobo and Pidgin English. Children from different ethnic nationalities communicate at school and in playgrounds with Pidgin English. With this socialization and peer pressure, children tend to speak more of Pidgin English and brand fellow speakers of Urhobo "*oburhobo*," bush people. It is very common in Effurun and Warri for Urhobo parents to speak only Pidgin English to their children or mix it with simple Urhobo. This aversion to Urhobo is largely because of the Western education of parents and their children. These parents also do not take their children to their traditional homes, where Urhobo is the only spoken language, a fact that would have forced the young ones to learn the language. The parents fear witchcraft and the unsanitary conditions in rural areas. Less contact with the traditional roots leads to less or no proficiency in Urhobo and the resort to speaking of Pidgin English. It was only during the Nigerian Civil War (1967-70) that there was a mass exodus from the cities such as Warri and Sapele to ancestral homes of the urbanites. It is remarkable that many of the young at that time credit their speaking and understanding Urhobo to their living in their rural towns and villages.

While the lingua franca status of Pidgin English erodes the currency of Urhobo, it absorbs many Urhobo words into it. Much of the Pidgin English spoken in Warri and Sapele, especially by the older people, appears to be literal translations from Urhobo. Expressions like "Carry go", "Not me and you" and "They born you throw way", for instance, are direct translations from Urhobo. Thus, much of Pidgin English has an Urhobo subtext. Pidgin English has absorbed some Urhobo words such as "*gbreghe*," "*ikebe*," "*ukodo*," and many others. This indicates the two-way traffic two languages interact, both influencing the other. In fact, many who speak Pidgin English use such Urhobo words without knowing.

Conclusion

The development of the Urhobo language is more self-assured today than twenty or more years ago because of the factors and trends already discussed. There is currently a self-conscious aspect to the evolution of the language. Many scholars of Urhobo, as at Delta State University and Urhobo Historical Society, are focusing on the Urhobo language in their research. This will result in more and more discussion of the language in its spoken and written aspects at an intellectual level. A few poets, including Atibọrọkọ Uyovbukherhi and the writer, have written modern poems in Urhobo. Students are studying the language and literature and doing their final year projects on relevant topics in the field. The Departments of English and Literary Studies and Languages and Linguistics (that houses the Urhobo Studies Programme) of Delta State University are at the forefront in the dissemination of knowledge in and about Urhobo. Graduates of the programme will in their works expose to the public the academic side of the language.

While the self-conscious scholarly side of "regulating" the language is going on, it is the people whose experiences find expression in the language that keep it evolving. A language evolves as it is used in the home and street as well as in written form by writers. Urhobo is only beginning to be employed in its modern totality. There is increasing expansion of the language as the people's experiences embrace the multifarious facets of contemporary living. The evolution of Urhobo language is coterminous with the evolution of the Urhobo society. A gradual shedding of "Aka" (Bini) has been taking place for centuries, as migration route experience, permanent neighbours, the environment, coming of Europeans, colonialism, modernity, and independent Nigerian rule, Urhobo national character, and other internal socio-cultural dynamics have helped to bring the language to its present state. Urhobo language is adapting to globalization and other new experiences. Backed by an academic institution and zealous literary and linguistic scholars and artists, the language is prepared to meet challenges of the future.

References and works cited

Alagoa, Ebiegberi, *A History of the Niger Delta*, Ibadan: Ibadan UP, 1972.

Awoonor, Kofi, *Guardians of the Sacred Word: Ewe Poetry*, New York: NOK, 1974.

Aziza, R.O., "Urhobo Tone System," PhD thesis, University of Ibadan, 1997.

Darah, G.G., "Language and Urhobo National Identity: A Review of Ayemenokpe Osubele's *A Dictionary of Urhobo Language*," unpublished essay (2003).

---. Ed., *Studies in Art, Religion & Culture Among the Urhobo and Isoko People*, Port Harcourt (2003).

Elugbe, B.O., *Comparative Edoid: Phonology and Lexicon, Delta Series No. 6*, Port Harcourt: University of Port Harcourt Press, 1989.

Diop, Chiekh Anta, *The African Origin of Civilization: Myth of Reality*, New York: Lawrence Hill, 1974.

Ikime, Obaro, *Niger Delta Rivalry: Itsekiri-Urhobo Relations and the European Presence, 1884—1936*, London: Longman, 1969.

Ojaide, Tanure, *Poetry, Performance, and Art: Udje Dance Songs of the Urhobo People*, Durham, NC: Carolina Academic Press, 2003.

---. With S. S. Ugheteni, *Yono Urhobo*, Lagos: Macmillan, 1983.

Opland, Jeff, *Xhosa Oral Poetry: Aspects of a black South African tradition*, Johannesburg: Ravan, 1983.

Otite, Onigu (ed), *The Urhobo People*, Ibadan: Heinemann, 1983.

Williamson, K., *Practical Orthography in Nigeria*, Ibadan, Heinemann, 1984.

2

The functions of tone in Urhobo and the need for tone-marking in the writing system

– Rose Aziza

Introduction

Urhobo is a southwestern *Edoid* language spoken extensively in Delta State, Nigeria. Like most Nigerian languages, it is a tone language. In general terms, tone refers to pitch differences, which occur usually at the level of the syllable. It is used to differentiate word meanings or convey or signal grammatical distinctions. It is a relative affair; that is, it is not something to be measured in absolute terms.

A tone language has been defined by Pike (1948) as one that has lexically significant contrastive but relative pitch on each syllable while Welmers (1959) has defined it as a language in which both pitch phonemes and segmental phonemes enter into the composition of at least some morphemes. Welmers' definition emphasizes the distinctive characteristics of a tone language as one in which some of its morphemes contain both segmental and pitch phonemes.

Urhobo has the type of tone system, which is classified as the terraced level tone system. In this type of tone system, a high tone at the end of an utterance is lower than one at the beginning because any intervening low tone has a lowering effect on the following non-low tone. This means that if we have a H – L – H – L – H sequence, each high tone after a low tone is realized a step lower than a preceding high tone although all the high tones are phonologically identical. Consequently the first high tone in the utterance is the highest pitch after which there may be a successive lowering of other high tones but there is never a return from a low tone to the pitch level of a preceding high tone. This successive lowering of high tones after low tones is referred to as downdrift or automatic downstep.

Urhobo tone system has the following characteristics:

a) Two basic tones, namely, the low tone and the high tone; these can be found in any position in an utterance-initially, medially or finally;
b) two gliding tones, namely, high – low (falling) and low – high (rising) which are derived from the basic tones;
c) a non-automatic downstep which is found only after the high tone;
d) only vowel segments bear tones.

The tones are indicated as follows:

High tone	=	H	=	[/]		
Low tone	=	L	=	[\ ]		
Downstep	=	!H	=	DS	=	[-]

Functions of tone in Urhobo

Tone has both lexical and grammatical functions. We shall, therefore, make a distinction between lexical and grammatical tones.

Lexical tones

Lexical tones are those borne by lexical items and are similar in function to vowel and consonant segments. A difference in tone can result in a difference in the meaning of otherwise homophonous words. Let us consider the following minimal pairs.

1.	(a)	ùkpè	year	úkpè	bed
		L L		H L	
	(b)	ọgọ	bottle	ọgọ	in-law
		L H		H DS	
	(c)	ènì	elephant	èní	head pad
		L L		L H	
	(d)	òdìbò	servant/slave	ódìbó	banana
		L L L		H L H	

The examples above show that the tones that each word bears cannot be ignored if the meanings of the words are to be realised.

In addition, nouns in Urhobo can be classified according to their tone patterns. Most nouns are either disyllabic or trisyllabic. On the basis of the patterning of the three pitch levels identified for the language, we can classify disyllabic nouns in their citation form into five tone groups as follows:

2. *Disyllabic nouns*

    Group 1:   High – High (H H) Nouns
    a) *ùkó*   cup
    b) *ọgba*   hero

    Group 2:   High Downstep (H DS) Nouns
    a) *ọgọ*   in-law
    b) *íghō*   money

    Group 3:   High – Low (H L) Nouns
    a) *ọgbàn*   thirty
    b) *úkpè*   bed

    Group 4:   Low – High (L H) Nouns
    a) *ọgọ*   bottle
    b) *ẹvwé*   goat

    Group 5:   Low – Low (L L) Nouns
    a) *ọgban*   horn
    b) *ẹvwè*   kola nut

Similarly, trisyllabic nouns can be classified into ten tone groups as follows:

3. *Trisyllabic nouns*

    Group 1:   High – High – High (H H H) Nouns
    a) *ágádá*   machete
    b) *ọmọmọ*   childish

    Group 2:   High – High – Downstep (H H DS) Nouns
    a) *órérē*   town
    b) *úkókō*   association, meeting

    Group 3:   High – High – Low (H H L) Nouns
    a) *ónógbò*   pussy cat
    b) *ítábà*   tobacco

    Group 4:   High – Low – High (H L L) Nouns
    a) *ódìbó*   banana
    b) *Ọghẹnẹ*   God

24 The Urhobo language today

Group 5: High – Low – Low (H L L) Nouns
a) ọshàrè — man
b) égòdò — compound

Group 6: Low – High – High (L H H) Nouns
a) ìrhíbó — pepper
b) òrúrú — thread

Group 7: Low – High – Downstep (L H DS) Nouns
a) ògbéyīn — tortoise
b) ùkútā — stone

Group 8: Low – High – Low (L H L) Nouns
a) ìdjérhè — road
b) ùtéhrù — iron

Group 9: Low – Low – High (H L L) Nouns
a) èghèdé — needle
b) òkpètú — trouble

Group 10: Low – Low – Low (L L H) Nouns
a) òdìbò — slave/servant
b) òhọrè — neck

Apart from the noun class, most adjectives and adverbs, which are derived from verbs, display particular tone patterns. Disyllabic adverbs usually bear the tones L H while trisyllabic ones bear the tones L H L as in the following examples:

4. Adverbs

    a) krẹkrẹn — shortish
    b) bièbí — blackish
    c) hẹhẹrè — wide
    d) miòmióvwì — ugly

Derived adjectives usually have a vowel prefix so that most of them have three or four syllables. Such adjectives with three syllables bear the tones H H L and those with four syllables bear the tones H H L L as in the following:

5. Adjectives

    a) ọfuáfò — white
    b) óbiébì — black
    c) ọrhórhòrhò — hot
    d) ódjídjìrò — cold

The few examples given above show that tone has a very important part to play in the make-up of lexical items in this language and so cannot be ignored.

Grammatical tones

Grammatical tones are those tones, which are grammatically significant and, within the autosegmental framework of generative phonology, they exist independently of 'segmental' phonological strings. They are mapped onto specific positions in the grammatical constructions in which they feature and affect the tonal output of the strings in the surface form. Tone exerts a lot of influence on the grammar of Urhobo as most of the grammatical information available is revealed through the manipulation of tones. For instance, most tense and aspectual information are indicated by tones. The segmentalisation of these grammatical tones usually results in the modification of lexical tones borne by adjacent segments. We shall consider a few of them.

Tone in the associative noun phrase

The associative construction is also called the Noun + Noun phrase. This construction is indicated by a morpheme /rẹ/ which bears a high tone and occurs between the two nouns. In normal conversational speech, the vowel of this associative marker (AM) is always elided but its high tone remains and gets relinked on the prefix vowel of the following noun and this results in tonal modifications on the second noun. Let us consider a few examples:

6. a) ùdì   +   rẹ   +   àyè   -[ùdi ráyè]
       L L   H   L L   [   ]
       drink   AM   woman   a woman's drink
    b) ìrhíbó +   rẹ   +   ínónẹ   [ìrhíbó rínónẹ]
       L H H   H   L H L   [   ]
       pepper   AM   today   today's pepper
    c) òzé   +   rẹ   +   íghō   [òzé ríghō]
       L H   H   H DS   [   ]
       basin   AM   money   a basin of money
    d) ékpù   +   rẹ   +   òrhuẹ   [ekpu rorhuẹ]
       H L   H   L H   [   ]
       bag   AM   hunter   a hunter's bag

From the examples above, we notice that while the first nouns in each phrase retain their lexical tones, the prefix vowels of the second nouns are all realised on the high tone given them by the associative marker. Consequently, examples 6(a), (b) and (d) whose second nouns in their citation form begin with a low tone become high because the high tone of the associative market relinks on their prefix vowel. Thus, we have a tonal modification from low to high. In 6(c), because the second noun already bears a high tone, no tonal modification takes place because the two high tones merely contract into one high tone.

Tone in the verb phrase

Most simple verbs in Urhobo are either monosyllabic or disyllabic and begin with a consonant segment. There are no minimal pairs in the verb class, which differ in meaning only as a result of a difference in tone patterning. So whereas we can classify nouns according to their tone patterns, verbs cannot be so classified. In the citation form, all verbs and all monosyllabic subject and object pronouns are realised on the low tone. Although a number of tonal alternations are attested in the verb, these are usually motivated by the different grammatical configurations in which they function. Consequently, all verbs with the same syllable structure will behave alike in the same grammatical configuration. For example, all monosyllabic verbs will behave alike in terms of tone in a past tense construction and all disyllabic verbs will also behave alike. For reasons such as these, Urhobo verbs as well as monosyllabic subject and subject pronouns are assumed to be underlyingly toneless and receive tone depending on the grammatical configuration in which they function. As a result, tone bears a great syntactic functional load particularly in the verb phrase. In order to be able to analyse tonal alternations in the Urhobo verb phrase, it is necessary to recognise the existence of tonal morphemes (tomorphs) or grammatical tones as an essential part of the grammar. These tomorphs may be single tone units or tonal melodies, that is, fixed tonal patterns, which are grammatically significant and exist independently of segmental strings. They are quite distinct from lexical tones. They are obligatorily segmentalised in appropriate positions within the grammatical configuration and their segmentalisation often causes lexical tones to delink or at best form a glide.

In this section, we shall consider grammatical constructions in the three basic tenses, namely, the present, the past and the future tenses.

The present tense

The present tense construction in Urhobo is used to convey a habitual as well as a present or continuous action. The morpheme marking the tense is a floating high tone, which occurs at the end of the subject noun phrase. In order for this tomorph to be realised, the final vowel of the subject noun phrase is lengthened slightly to accommodate it. If the subject NP already ends on a high tone, it is easy to perceive a lengthening of both the high tone and the final vowel. If on the other hand, if the subject NP ends on a low tone, the present tense tomorph is segmentalised on the lengthened portion of the final vowel. We said earlier that when the subject pronoun or verb is not bearing a tomorph, it is realised on a low tone. Consequently, if the subject NP is a pronoun, the first part of the vowel bears a low tone while the lengthened portion bears the high tone. Let us examine some examples. (Note: pr.t= present tomorph.)

7. a) Ẹsè + / + dẹ   + ọbe = ẹsèé   dØ ọbe   =
       H L + (H) + L   L L   H L H   Ø L L
       Name Pr.t buy   book
       [ẹsèé dọbe]
       H LH L L   'Ese buys/ is buying a book'

   b) Éjìró + /   +   shẹ   +   íkó   =
       H L H   (H)   L   H H
       Name   Pr.t   sell   cups
       Éjìróó   shØ   íko   =   [Éjìróó shíko]
       H LHH   Ø   HH   H LHH   H H
                                         'Ejiro is selling/sells cups'

   c) Ọ + /   dà   + ùdì   =   ọọ   dØ   ùdi = [ọọ dùdì]
       L (H) L   L L   L H Ø   L L   L H LL
       Subj.pron. pr.t (alcoholic) drink 'he / she drinks/is drinking

The past tense

In the full form of the past tense, the verb appears with a suffix, which is realised in two phonological shapes depending on the vowel harmony requirements of the verb stem vowel. (Vowels in this language fall into two groups with regard to vowel harmony and the harmony feature is the Advanced Tongue Root [ATR]). Consequently, the vowels /i, e, o, u,/ are [+ATR] while /ẹ, a, ọ/ are [-ART]. For a detailed discussion of vowel harmony in Urhobo, see Aziza (1994, 1997)). The alternating forms of the verb suffix are – ri and re. If the verb stem vowel is [+ ATR], it takes the suffix –ri but if the verb stem is [-ATR], it takes –re. This suffix occurs only when the verb is not followed by an object; where it is, the suffix is deleted.

As for tonal alternation, the past tense construction assigns a high tomorph, which is segmentalised on the only vowel segment of a monosyllabic verb stem or on the final vowel of a disyllabic verb stem. When the verb stem is followed by a noun object, the final vowel of the verb stem is either elided or undergoes glide formation resulting in the past tense tomorph being set afloat. Since it is a grammatical tone, it obligatory relinks on the prefix vowel of the following noun object resulting in the delinking of the lexical tone in that position if it is a low. However if it is a high, it contracts with the high tomorph and so the effect of the relinking is vacuous. Let us consider some examples:

a) Ẹsè   dẹrè   =   [Ẹsè dẹrè]
   H L   H L   H L H L
   Name bought   'Ese bought'

b) Éjìró   shérì   =   [Éjìró shérì]
   H LH   H L   H L H H L
   Name fell down   'Ejiro fell down'

c) Àyè nà tòrhẹ ùwèvwìn   =   [Àyè nà tòrhẹ ùwèvwìn]
   L L L L H L L L   L L L L H L L
   Woman the burnt house   'The woman burnt a house'

d) ọmọ dẹ ọnẹ   =   [ọmọ dọnẹ]
   H H H L H   H H H H
   child bought yam   '(a) child bought yam'

e) Ẹsè fọrhọn ébò   =   [Ẹsè fọrhébò]
   H L L H   H L   H L L H L
   Name washed sack   'Ese washed a sack'

The future tense

In its full form, the future tense is marked segmentally by a particle, which occurs between the subject noun phrase and the verb stem of the clause. This particle is realised in two phonological shapes /che/ and /cha/ depending on the vowel harmony requirement of the verb stem vowel. If the verb stem vowel is [+ART], it selects /che/ and if it is [-ART], it selects /cha/. This future tense is used to indicate an action that is yet to commence or one that is being contemplated.

Tonally, the future tense construction is marked by a H – L – H tone sequence which is distributed as follows:
    a) the first high tone is segmentalised on the final vowel of the subject noun phrase (or the only vowel segment of a monosyllabic subject pronoun).
    b) the low tone is mapped onto the future tense particle, and
    c) the second high tone is mapped onto the only or first vowel of the verb stem and spreads onto any following vowel segment within the verb stem; hence, all verb stem vowels are realised as high. We shall consider some examples:

9. a) Ọ   chà   dẹ   =   [Ọ chà dẹ]
       H   L   H   H   L   H
       He/she particle   buy   'he/she will buy'

    b) Ó   chè   chéré   =   [Ó chè chéré]
       H   L   H H   H   L   H H
       He/she particle cook   S (He) will cook

    c) Ẹsé   chà   gháré ọnẹ =   [Ẹsé chà ghárọnẹ]
       H H   L   H H L H   H H L   H H H
       Name   part.   share yam   'Ese will share yam'

    d) Éjìró   chè   sí   ọbe   =   [Éjìró chè siọbe]
       H LH   L   H   L L   H LH L   H L
       Name part. write book   'Ejiro will write a book/letter'

The examples above show that tonal alternations in this construction result from the segmentalisation of the two high tones marking the future tense. The segmentalisation of the first high tone onto the subject NP results in the automatic delinking of the inherent or lexical tone in that position if it is low. (This is unlike what happens with the present tomorph whose segmentalisation results in the lengthening of the final vowel of the subject NP so as to accommodate the tomorph.) The second high tone of the future tense spreads onto other vowel segments within the verb stem if the verb stem is other than monosyllabic. It is unlike the past tense tomorph, which does not spread. However like the past tense tomorph, if the final vowel of the verb stem is elided or becomes a glide, this tomorph obligatorily relinks and the result is automatic delinking of a following inherent tone. In each case, the effect of segmentalisation is vacuous if the inherent tone is also a high.

Negation and interrogation

Negation in Urhobo is marked by a floating L H tone sequence, which is mapped onto the final vowel in the phonetic realisation. In order to accommodate the tone sequence, the final vowel is lengthened. In the orthography this is represented by doubling the final vowel. Thus we have the following:

10. a) Ẹsè   dẹ   ọnẹ   \ /   =   [Ẹsè dọnẹẹ]
       H L   H   L H   (LH)   H L   H HLH
       Name bought yam   negative   'Ese did not buy yam'

b) Ọ   shẹ   ùdì   \/   =   [Ọ   shúdìí]
    L   H   L L   (LH)   L   H LH
    He / She sold (alcoholic) drink Neg.   S(He) did not sell a drink

On the other hand, interrogation is marked by a floating low tone, which is realised on the final vowel of the utterance. If the statement already ends on a low tone, the addition of this question morpheme results in our perceiving the utterance on an extra low level. However, if the statement ends on a high tone the addition of the question morpheme results in the creation of a HL contour but there is no lengthening of the final vowel. The following are some examples:

11. a) Ọ   shẹ   ùdi   \   =   [ọ   shùdi]
       L   H   L L   (L)   L   H L
       he sold drink   Question   'Did he sell a drink?'

    b) Ẹsè   dẹ   ọnẹ   \   =   [Ẹsè   dọnẹ]
       H L   H   L H   (L)   H L   H HL
       Name bought yam Question   'Did Ese buy yam?'

From the foregoing, it is clear that tone has both lexical and grammatical functions in Urhobo and that it is as important, if not even more important, than the consonant and vowel segments used in utterances.

The need for tone-marking in the writing system

We decided to give a technical treatment to our section 3 in order to show that tone in Urhobo is not just a matter of choice or something that is haphazardly done but that it is a systematic phenomenon which is well entrenched in the grammar of the language. Tone can differentiate the meaning of words as well as distinguish different grammatical constructions.

A number of people object to the use of tone marks in writing simply because it is not used in English and so they consider it untidy. They seem to forget that English is not a tone language in the sense that Urhobo is. Whether you say 'clear' with a high, mid or low tone, the meaning is the same in English. But as we have seen, a change in tone can change the meaning of words in Urhobo. If tone is not marked in writing many sentences would be ambiguous and a lot of time and meaning would be lost.

Some people claim that tone marking is unnecessary because the context can always make the meaning clear. But this is not always true. For example,"*me mrẹ ẹvwe*". This sentence could mean either "I saw a goat" or "I saw kolanut". Just relying on context will not make the meaning of the above sentence clear, and there are many such sentences in Urhobo. We need the tone marks to make reading easier, clearer and more interesting.

The three pitch levels identified in Urhobo could be marked in the orthography as follows:

    a)   High tone   =   /

    b)   Low tone   =   \

    c)   Downstep   =   ——

(Note that the downstep is marked as though it is a mid tone but it should be remembered that it is not a proper mid tone.)

Consequently, we can distinguish the three sentences below easily:

16. a) Àyè nà dẹ àmwá   'The woman bought a cloth'

    b) Àyè nă dẹ àmwá   'The woman is buying a cloth'

    c) Àyè nâ dẹ àmwá   'The woman would buy a cloth'

However, having established that we need to mark tones in the writing system, the question now is, how much tone marking is necessary? We have seen that words can be distinguished by tone but some of these words tend to change their tones when they occur in sentences. In addition, there are important grammatical constructions, which are distinguished only by tone. For these reasons, we agree with the recommendation in Manual V of the *Orthographies of Nigerian Languages* that only the high tone and the downstep need to be marked. The low tone should be left unmarked in the writing system. This is also a kind of spelling rule such that any vowel that does not bear a tone mark is pronounced on the low tone.

Conclusion

We have tried to demonstrate the important role tone plays in Urhobo and to advocate the need for marking tone in the writing system.

It is hoped that lecturers, students and writers in Urhobo will become more interested in marking tone so as to make our writing more accurate and less ambiguous.

References

Aziza, R. O. (1994): "Vowel Harmony in Urhobo," *Nigerian Language Studies*. No. 2: 1–7

Aziza, R. O. (1997): Urhobo Tone System," PhD thesis, University of Ibadan.

Elugbe, B. O. (1989): *Comparative Edoid: Phonology and Lexicon*, Delta Series No. 6, University of Pot Harcourt Press.
Elugbe, B. O. (1991): "The Limits of Accuracy in the Design of Orthographies". *JWAL* XXI: 49 – 54.
Federal Ministry of Education, *Orthographies of Nigerian Languages,* Manual V
Goldmith, j. (1976):"Autosegmental Phonology," PhD thesis, M.I.T. Massachusetts.
Kelly, J. (1969): "Urhobo" in E. Dunstan (ed.), *Twelve Nigerian Languages.* London: Longman, 153 – 161.
Pike, K. L. (1948*): Tone Languages.* Ann Arbor: University of Michigan Press.
Welmers, W. E. (1959): "Tonemics, Morphotonemics and Tonal Morphemes," *General Linguistics,* 4: 1 – 9.
Welmers, W. E. (1969): "Structural Notes on Urhobo," *JWAL* 6 (2): 85 – 107.
Williamson, K. (1984): *Practical Orthography in Nigeria,* Ibadan: Heinemann.

3

Lexis and structure in Urhobo

– Igho J. Onose

This topic can be examined within the two areas of the noun phrase and the verb phrase in the language. There are all kinds of nouns and structures within the noun phrase.

Classes of nouns

Simple noun

The class of simple nouns embraces names of persons, places and objects. As regards the names of persons, it must be stressed that most names in Urhobo are either phrasal or sentential nouns. They are not what one could ordinarily call simple lexical items. They express a fact rather than simply, name. They can, however, be accepted, and in fact, are regarded as simple names, just as such English names as Miss Edith Sitwell, Newfoundland, gas cooker and record player are categorised.

The Urhobo names in question are such names as:

1. 'Mudiaga' (stand firm)

Others include:

2. Onojìghẹgùọnọ (who does not like money?)
   Ọmọnìgho (child is better than money)
   Ọmọtẹkoro (a daughter is golden)
   Ovwùghẹghẹwariotà (He who mocks someone else's misfortune is a fool)

The names of places such as:
3. Okparà
   Ekù

34 The Urhobo language today

      Ovu
      Ovwahwa
also belong to the category of simple nouns. There are also names of objects such as.

  4.   *imèjẹ*   table
       ọfigbo   oil
       ìmóto   car/lorry
       èbị   leaf/book
       oda   cutlass
in this group.

Colour adjectives

Such adjectival words/ *bịèbi/* 'black', /*fúànfụ*/ 'white' can be used as nouns. This type of adjective is what Strang calls colour adjectives. According to Strang, colour adjectives are like adjectives in all positive respects, but in addition, they take on sentence – functions of nouns, i.e. occurring as subject, etc.

Examples of colour adjectives, which take on sentence functions, are:

  5.   *Ọfúánfụ* 'white' and *óbièbi* 'black' as they occur in the sentences that follow:

  6.   *Ófuánfụ na*   *jěvwè*
      White   the   please me
      i.e. 'I like the white'

  7.   *Mị guọnọ*   *óbiebi na*
      I want + pres   black   the
      i.e. 'I want the black'

As colour words are not many in this language, it is not possible to cite many examples.

A second type of nouns which is probably best seen as a 'colour adjective' functioning as a noun is very much more abstract than the category just described. This latter kind is formed by a change in the prefix vowel associated with the basic colour terms discussed earlier on. Thus from *Ọfùanfụ* 'white' we have *ófuánfụ* 'whiteness'; similarly from *óbièbi* 'black' we have *ùbièbi* 'blackness'.

That this is the case is evident in the fact that the example below is in fact an acceptable sentence in Urhobo.

  8   *Ubiebi*   *yóónma*
     blackness   be +pres   good
     i.e. 'blackness is good'

They are essentially instances of the abstract noun.

De-adjectival class nouns

These nouns are formed from adjectives. Thus, an expression such as:

9.   *Irėdiȧ*   *Ovwiėgbėre*
         Iredia   poor person
        i.e. 'Iredia is poor /Iredia is a poor person.'

is an example.

The ways in which the above sentence and other similar comparable sentences in Urhobo are used and interpreted, clearly indicate that *ovwiėgbėre* 'poor person' in such sentences is construed as either an adjective or as a noun. The gloss provided for the example cited here is intended to reflect this state of affairs. Other items that behave like *ovwiėgbėre* in Urhobo would include *ọdafị* 'rich (person)' and its plural counterpart *edafị*.

Other examples are:

10.   *Ȯchȋbẹ*   impotent
       ȯgbȯtȧ   talkative

Temporal adverbs

Like locative adverbs in Urhobo, temporal adverbs sometimes function as nouns. Welmers recognized this fact when he noted that 'the locative expression themselves are nouns.' As nouns they take the definite determiner /na/.

Consider in this connection:

11   *Nȯnẹ*   na   *grȯri*
    Today   the   long
    i.e. 'Today is long'

12. *Ukpe*   na   *yȯȯnma*
    year   the   good
    i.e. 'The year is good'

Locative adverbs

Nouns of this class have to do with descriptions involving space. This refers to such spaces as 'inside the house', 'under the tree' etc.

Appropriate examples include:

13. *ȯtọrutiė*   na   *djirȯri*
    under of orange-tree   the   cool
    i.e. 'It is cool under the orange tree'

14. Evunrůwenvwin   na   vwȧ   rhụarhủ
    Inside of the house the   be + pres.   spacious
    i. e. 'the house is spacious'

Here, the expression *evunrůwenvwin na* functions as the subject.

Deverbal nouns

Nouns of this class are formed from verbs by prefixing a specific vowel to a verb stem. As nouns they can occur in subject, object or complement positions. These nominalizations include such words as.

15.   ůse   calling
        orẹ   begging
        ȯyȧn   walking
        ẹrȧ   going
        ẹchȧ   coming
        enė   defeacating

16. O   nyȯ   ůse   mė
     he   hear + past   calling   my
     i.e. 'he heard my calling'
     ůse mė functions as the object.

Also ȯyȧn   rọyịn
      Walking   of him
         i.e. 'his walking'
functions as subject in:

17. ȯyȧn   rọyịn   vwa   kpatapata
    walking   of him   be + pres   very fast
    i.e. 'His walking is very fast'

Like in Yoruba, some nouns are formed by the addition of prefixes /ọ/ and /o/ to verbs or verb-nominal compounds. This results in a class of nominal, which often means 'one that does ...'"

18   -vwịọmọ   (bring forth a child)
     ȯvwiọmọ   (one who brings forth children)
     -suotȧ   (cause trouble)
     ọsuotȧ   (one who causes trouble)
     -bru orhiė   (decide a case)
     ȯbrorhien   (one who decides cases)

In the same way /ọbủ/ added to nominal items forms new words.

19. -une song
    ọbú + úne 'one who sings/lead singer'
    ọ̀búúne
    osio 'rain'
    ọ̀bú + ọsio rain maker'
    ọbúosio
    evwá 'oracle'
    ọbú + évwa 'diviner'
    ọbuevwá

Another item, which is prefixed to nominal items to form other nouns, is Ògbá strong/strongman/good at.
Thus:

20 Ogbá +ówian   ógbówian   'strong labourer'
    ógbá + avwrụ   ọgbávwrụ   'one who argues much'
    ọgbá + ikọkọ   ọgbikọkọ   'A stammerer'
    ọgbá + otá   ọgbotá   'one who talks much'

Another class of nouns called abstract nouns in traditional grammar usually refers to non-tangible things, thoughts and concepts. These are such noun as hope and length. In Urhobo abstract nouns are formed by prefixing a specific vowel to verbal stems. Examples of such nouns in Urhobo are:

21 verbs   Noun formed
    /roro/   think   /iroro/thought
    /guọnọ/ like/love   /ẹgúọnọ/ love
    /kugbe/ come together   /okugbé/ togetherness
    /yan/   walk   /oyan/walking
    /fi/   leak   /efio/leakage

Looking at the examples, one is inclined to point out that a factor that determines the choice of a prefix for the formation of abstract nouns from verbal stems has to do with vowel patterning along the close/open dichotomy. For example, in /iroro/ the choice of the /i/ a close vowel as a prefix has to do with the other vowels in the verb stem which too are in the close class. This argument also is valid for the choice of /ẹ/ as a prefix for /ẹguọnọ/. Vowel harmony is very much at work here.

The next class is a collection of concepts/objects of the same nature. In Urhobo, these are also formed by prefixing a specific vowel to a verbal stem.

22 Verb   Noun formed
    /koko/ come together   /ùkóko/club, meeting
    /krun/load/parcel   /ekrun/a pack
    /krun/gather together   /ėkrun/family/bunch
    /ghwėkoko/come together   /ǫghwękokó/a gathering

Another class of nouns is characteristically not pluralisable. Such nouns in the language include the following:

23. eyagha   cassava flour
     igarị   garri
     ėkpę   sand
     amị   water

The formation of the next class of noun involves some morphological processes with the specific noun. For example:
ayị 'woman' is reduplicated and inserted in the structure.

24.   ki...ki...as
             ki ayi ki ayi   [kaji kaji]
             ki ayi ki ayi   whatever/whichever/every/any woman
             ki ǫmǫ ki ǫmǫ   Whatever/whichever/every/any child
             ki ohwȯ ki ohwȯ   whatever/ whichever/every/any person

The first instance of this duplication ends in a high tone for a disyllabic word even if the word originally belongs to the LL group. This is illustrated by ayi above. In a disyllabic word with HH or LH the first instance retains the high tone finally.

Two other linguistic forms, which for classificatory purposes should be mentioned because they are dominated by the NP node, are nominalizations and relative clauses.

Nominalizations

These are sentential structures, which are transformationally derived and are capable of existing under the NP node. To this extent they can be called sentential noun phrases. In most case they are introduced by any of the complementizers.

25.   nị   'that'
            tanị   'that'

in the Urhobo language. Nominalizations can occur in all the positions indicated earlier for a noun phrase. An example would be:

26. Nị   wọ   wan   ọdavwini
    wèn   yóònma
    that   you   pass +past   examination   you   good
    i.e. 'that you passed your examination is good.'

As well as occurring in the subject position, the noun phrase can be moved to object position by a transformational process of extraposition.

27. O yóònma   tảnị   wọ   wản   odavwinì   wẹn
    it be + pres good that you   pass + past examination your
    i.e.   'it is good that you passed your examination'

The relative clause

The other structure that is capable of appearing under the NP node is the relative clause. In the words of Stockwell et al 'A sentence embedded as a modifier of an NP, the embedded sentence having within it a WH pronominal replacement for a deep structure NP which is in some sense identical with the head NP, is a relative clause.'

In Urhobo the relative pronoun or WH pronominal that introduces the relative clause is *ri/ri*.

This *ri/ri* assumes many forms because of the influence of assimilation. An example of a relative clause in Urhobo is:

28 oze   ri   mi   dẹrị   na   kpọkpọrị
    basin   which   I   buy + past the   be + pres.   new
    i.e. 'the basin which I bought is new'

Nouns in Urhobo can therefore be said to have two sources. The point has been made earlier that there are nouns, which are generated in the base while some others are derived transformationally. Those generated at the base are such nouns as:

29   ůkẻ   -   egg
            óhọ   -   hen
            osa   -   debt
            isọn   -   excrement/excreta
            ọmợ   -   off – spring

These words listed above can combine transformationally with other nominals or proforms to yield other nominals like the ones listed below:

30	ukọ́nhọ	-	egg of a hen
	isọnhọ	-	droppings of a hen
	ọrìesa	-	debtor
	ọ̀mọ́họ	-	chick

Thus, the noun phrase has been shown to embrace quite a large number of entities (exhibiting unique features) such as names of persons, objects, places and concepts such as *omemuovwiyo*-'sadness'- and *omavwerhovwe*- 'happiness.' The noun in Urhobo can also be replaced by the pronoun. Like in English we can itemize the pronouns in a pronominal system as follows:

31. Singular (Subject)

1st pers.	mị/mi	as in	mị ria
2nd pers.	wọ/wo	" "	wọ ria
3rd pers.	ọ/o	" "	ọ ria

Singular (Object)

1st pers.	vwẹ/vwe	as in	ọ ga vwẹ
2nd pers.	wẹwe	" "	ọ ga wẹ
3rd pers.	rọ/ro	as in	ọ ga rọ

32. Plural (Subject)

1st pers.	Ohwo (inclusive)
	Ma/Avwarị (exclusive)
2nd pers.	Wa
3rd pers.	ayi
	Plural (object)
1st pers.	Ohwo (inclusive)
	Avwarị (exclusive)
2nd pers.	owavwa
3rd pers	ayi

These pronouns when used emphatically can change morphologically as the following example show.

33. Subject singular

1st pers.	Ọmẹ	i.e.	it is I
2nd pers	Ọwẹ	i.e.	it is you
3rd pers.	Ọ̀yi	i.e.	it is he/she, it

Subject plural

1st pers.	ohwo	i.e.	it is we (inclusive)
	avwari	i.e.	it is we (exclusive)
2nd pers.	Owavwa	i.e.	it is you
3rd pers.	Ayi	i.e.	it is they.

Adjectives

These are words that qualify nouns. This means that they help to paint the nouns, which they qualify clearly. Adjectives in Urhobo are derived from verbs. Thus, from such verbs as:

34.
	bi	-	be black
	gro	-	be tall
	kre	-	be short
	rho	-	be big (fat)
	gbe	-	be dirty
	do̩	-	be thin

we form by way of morphological reduplication such adjectives as

biebi	-	black
grongro	-	tall
kre̩kre̩	-	short
rhuarho	-	big (fat)
gbegbe	-	dirty
do̩do̩	-	thin

A second category of adjectives though appears reduplicated morphologically is actually generated at the base. Such adjectives include such words as.

35.
	djidji	-	stupid
	rhurhu	-	stupid
	mimi	-	stupid
	kpokpan	-	thick
	tunotuno	-	small
	vweghevweghe	-	flat

Most forms, which are modifiers in the language, appear generated at the base and they include such ones as

phrejephreje	-	soft
gbingogbingo	-	very thin
kikiriki	-	stubby/strong

The definite determine '*na*' in Urhobo also acts as a modifier, it specifies the meaning of the noun that it goes with. An example is:

36. '*O̩mo̩ na cha*' which means 'the child is coming'. This is different from '*o̩mo cha*' which means '*A child is coming.*' The definite determiner is to be seen in such expressions as

37.   *Ayi̩ na*   -   The woman

Oshari na	-	The man
Eranko na	-	The dog

The indefinite article in Urhobo, however, generally has a zero realization. In other words, a noun not accompanied by any particular determiner is given either a generic or indefinite interpretation.

38.   Omo   yoma
      i.e. child (generic) is good .

Another
           kevvwe uko
    i.e.   Give me a cup (indefinite).

In certain contexts, however, the word *Ovu* (certain, some) expresses indefiniteness.
Consider, for example:

39.   Mi   mren   uko   ovu
      I   see + past cup   certain
      i.e. 'I saw a certain cup'.

One says that '*na*' (the) and *Ovu* (some, certain) are modifiers in the Urhobo language. A reduplicated form of '*na*' which is nana is used in place of *na* for emphasis. Consider:

40.   Omo   na   ome (The child is mine)
                    and
      Omo   nana   ome (This very child is mine)

The indefinite determiner (but not the definite) can be pluralized to agree in number with its head noun. An example

41   omo   ovu   a certain child
      emo   evu   some/ certain children
      Omo   na   the child
      emo   na   the children

Pre-nominal qualifier: These are qualifiers which precede the head noun and the /na/. This group includes such words as:

Omo	-	little/insignificant
Okpo	-	quite/substantial

as exemplified below:

42. *Omo   ota   na*
     little   talk   the
     i.e. 'the little talk'
     okpọ   ọkụ   na
     big   parcel   the
     i.e. the big parcel

Another group of modifiers that precede the head noun are the so called fractional quantifiers. The conjunctive 'rị' joins them to the noun.

43. *Ubro   ri   ọnẹ*   a piece of yam
     Ubro   ri   urhe   a piece of wood
     Ubro   ri   ibredi   a piece of bread

The Ubro 'piece' which occurs in the above phrases sometimes occurs without an associate noun head in what in terms of Halliday is probably described as a "... structure deictic head" (62) with a qualifier realizing the word as we find in

44. *Ubro   mi   rịrị*
     Half   I   eat + past
     i.e. "it is half that I ate."

The point to note about a sentence such as the above is that the referent of the noun qualified by *ubro* ('half') must be known to both speaker and hearer. The demonstrative adjectives discussed above have pronoun counterparts involving a prefix /Ọ/. They occur in the structures exemplified below:

45. *Ọna   (ọnana) ayẹ*   'this is a woman'
     ọna   (onana) ọmọ   'this is a child'
     Ọmọ   (ọ) vu   cha   -   a (certain) child is coming
     Ọvu   cha   -   a certain one is coming
     Ọmọ yena   cha   -   that child is coming
     Ọyena   cha   -   that one is coming

Demonstrative pronouns are pluralized in agreement with their deixes.

46   *Enana (ena) emẹ.*   These ones are mine
     Evu yooma   Some (certain ones) are good
     Eyena   eya   Those ones are woman.

These examples point to the existence of subject-complement agreement in Urhobo. This fact accounts for the unacceptability of:

47. *Oyena eya*   -   That is woman
     Eyina   ayi   -   Those are a woman

A careful consideration of noun phrases involving qualifiers and the determiner *na* as stated before, suggests that whereas certain qualifiers co-occurring with a noun and the determiner *na* 'the' tend to feature between the noun and the associated determiner (as in the examples:

48   *ayị*   *mẹ na*   'the my wife'
      ayị   *rẹsosuọ na*   'the first woman'
      ayị   *re mudia na*   ' the woman who is standing'

Some others occur phrase finally i.e. after the determiner *na*. The latter situation applies to quantifiers such as

49   *eeje /ejobi*   -   all
      ive   -   both / the two
      ọvuovuu   -   no / none of

as illustrated in:

50.   *emọ*   *na*   *eeje/ejobi*   -   all the children
      emọ   *na*   *ive*   -   the two/both children
      emọ   *na*   *ovuọvúú*   -   none of the children

Cardinal and multiplier qualifiers behave essentially like phrase final qualifiers. Thus cardinal and multiplier qualifiers in Urhobo occur after *na* in the noun phrase. This is illustrated in the examples that follow:

51   *ehọ*   *na*   *ivẹ*   -   the two hens
      ehọ   *na*   *erha*   -   the three hens

Here, the cardinals occur after the *na* in the noun phrase. Like the cardinals, the multipliers also occur after the determiner. Consider:

52.   *emu*   *na*   *aka*   *ivẹ*   *buru*
      food   the   place   two   enough
      i.e. the food in two places is enough

Evwe   *na*   *rhu*   *nẹ*   *ọhọ*   *na*   *aka*   *erha*
goat   the   big +pres   than   hen   the   place   three
      i.e.   'the goat is bigger in three places than the hen'
          'the goat is three times as big as the hen.'

The qualifiers *eeji/ejobi, ovuọvu* and the cardinals, ordinals and the fractional quantifiers sometimes occur in structures that are comparable to the sentence with *ubro* ('half') above. The point made with respect to *ubro* earlier would apply with equal validity to the underlined in the examples that follow:

53.   *eeje/ejobi rhoro*   -   all are big
      ovuọvu rhoro   -   none is big
      ẹne rhoro   -   four are big

esan rhoro	- six are big
orive na biri	- the second is black

Adjective qualifiers

Adjectives usually occur postponed to the nouns that they modify.

54. *Ohwo   grongro*   -   tall person
     ohwo   biebi   -   dark person

It is not unusual to find a string of adjectives within the same sentence in Urhobo. For instance, we find:

Aye	*ọvu*	*grongro,*	*biebi*	*rhuarho*
Woman	some	tall	dark	fat

i.e. 'some tall dark fat woman'

Adjectives in Urhobo can themselves be modified by intensifiers. This is the case in an example such as:

55. | *Ohwo* | *grongro* | *mamọ / gangan* |
     |--|--|--|
     | person | tall | very |

The two morphemes *mamọ* and *gangan* are intensifiers in Urhobo which mean 'very'. They can be used interchangeably.

The order of occurrence of adjectives does not appear to affect the grammaticality or otherwise of appropriate sentences in Urhobo. Consider:

56. | *ayị* | *biebi* | *rhuarho* | *grongro* |
     |--|--|--|--|
     | woman | dark | fat | tall |

and

ayi	*rhuarho*	*biebi*	*grongro*
woman	fat	dark	tall

i.e. 'A tall dark fat woman.'

Both expressions are acceptable, unlike in English where we talk of adjectives of age and colour and size, which are used in a definite order. The point is that in Urhobo this order does not seem to be important.

Genitival constructions in Urhobo

The genitival construction is the phrase of choice for expressing the idea of possession in Urhobo. Welmers points out that apart from the first and second person singular, possession involving the other pronouns and nouns in Urhobo is sometimes indicated by the use of genitive constructions. The genitival phrase involves the use of the conjunctive element *ri/re* as we find:

57.
Ọbe	mẹ		my book
Ọbe	wẹ		your book
Ọbe	ri	Davidi	David's book
Owo	ri	esi	leg of pig

Order of occurrence of qualifiers

When the different qualifiers attested in Urhobo occur together in a sentence the order of occurrence is usually as indicated below:

1. headword (noun)
2. adjective or numeral
3. numeral or adjective
4. relative clause
5. determiner
6. quantifier

The order of occurrence indicated above can be exemplified with.

58. Eshariị yonyonvwin iyonrin [rị a mren re] na eeje
    (1)   (2)   (3)   (4)   (5) (6)

    Eshariị iyonrin yonyonvwin [rị a mren re] na eeje
    (1)   (2)   (3)   (4)   (5) (6)

i.e. 'All the five handsome men that we saw.'

The verbal group

This is the group of words that usually occurs in the predicate position. It is a verb in an SV construction. Consider for example:

    59. *Ojo cha*   -   Ojo is coming
It is a verb and an object in an SVO construction. An example is:

    60. *Ojo hwẹ oghwokpo*   -   Ojo killed a toad
It is thus possible to talk of the intransitive and transitive verbs as already demonstrated.

Transitive verbs

These are verbs that take an object to make the sentence meaningful. Some of such verbs are:

61.
hwe	-	kill/beat
duvwu	-	stab/grind
mrẹ́n	-	see
da	-	drink
dẹ	-	buy
gua	-	ride/drive, pilot (vb).
re	-	eat
rị	-	beg
she	-	cut
hwerhe	-	sweep.

These verbs can be found in such expressions as:

Umukoro	hwẹ	ẹvwe
Umukoro	killed	a goat

62. Ọmọ na mrẹ̀n ọse rẹ̀ ọyịn   The child saw its father
    Ọnotu dả ame   -   Onotu drank water

The intransitive verbs, however, occur without the object. Some examples of the intransitive verb are:

63.
she	-	fall
vrẹ	-	stand
chidia	-	sit
ghwu	-	die
mọ	-	bear fruit / come
ya	-	walk
yara	-	go
vie	-	cry
vweroma	-	weep/mourn
ne	-	shit
vwe	-	piss

These, like others, can be used in sentences such as:

64.
Idogho sheri	-	Idogho fell
Onotu vrẹri	-	Onotu stood up
Evwe na ghwuru	-	The goat died
Utie na mọre	-	The orange tree bore fruits.
Mi ne	-	I am defeacating
Me vwe	-	I am urinating

An important grammatical phenomenon worth mentioning now, though deserving a special treatment elsewhere, is vowel harmony. It is to be noted that the phenomenon of vowel harmony is important in the Urhobo language. The simple past is formed by the addition of *ri* to the base form of the verb. This '*ri*' can change to '*rẹ*' with verbs the vowels of whose base forms are 'a ẹ ọ' while *ri* is for those verbs whose stem vowels are 'e o u'.

For example, the simple past form of *she* (fall) is *sheri* (fell) while that for *da* (drink) is *dare*.

The '*ri*' for *she* (fall) and '*re*' for *da* (drink) are chosen in conformity to the vowels of the base morphemes. This, however, is by the way.

Split verbs

These are verbs which are used serially or sequentially to express a single action. Example:

65. Orido   rie   emu (Orido ate)
     Orido   sherhẹ   (*Orido* lay down)
     Orirdo riẹ   emu   sherhẹ   (Orido ate and lay down

or

Orido ate before going to bed)

Here, two verbs, namely *rie emu* (ate) and *sherhe* (lay down/went to bed) are conflated to portray a single action.

Another example is:

66   Idọghọ   vreri   (Idogho got up)
     Idọghọ   mudia   (Idogho stood up)

The two verbs *vreri* and *mudia* can be brought together to portray a single action in:

67. Idọghọ   vre   mudia
     Idọghọ   get up + past   stand + past
     i.e. 'Idogho stood up.'

A third example is:

68. Okoro *mrẹn rị*   (Okoro saw or realised)
     Okoro *vugheri*   (Okoro knew)

These two verbs are serialized:

69. Okoro   mrẹn   vughe
     Okoro   see + past   know + past
     i.e. 'Okoro realised.'

In some cases, a nominal is inserted between such two verbs and (I think this is where the term "split verb" is more appropriate.) An example is:

70 Umukoro   jẹ   amị   (Umokoro served water)
    Umukoro   da   amị   (Umukoro drank water)

The two verbs 'served' and 'drank' are put together but separated by the nominal water as:

71 Ùmukòro   jè   amị   da.
    Ùmukòro serve + past   water drink + past
    i.e. Umokoro served and drank water.

Other examples of such verbs are:

72. Fi (leak through)   she (fall)   fishe (dropped)
     She (fall)   ghwru (be lost)   sheghwru (got lost)
     Ya (walk)   wan (go past)   yawan (walk past)
     mu (catch)   re (eat)   mure (catch and eat)
     suo (provide company)   kpo (go home)   suokpo (guard him home)
     bru (cut)   reyọ (take)   bru reyọ (cut and take)

Verbs in the language can be used to express actions that are past, present, progressive, habitual and future actions. Tense in the language is more a feature of phonology than of morphology. This is in the sense that tense is largely expressed phonologically by means of tones. A tonal change on the subject noun usually indicates the tense of the verb.

The present tense

The combination of the low and high tones on the pronominal indicates the simple present. Examples are:

73   Mi   kpè   eki   -   I am going to market
     Ò   dẹ̀   Udi   -   He is drinking

Past tense

In expressing the past tense the pronominal takes the low tone. Examples are:

74   Mì   kpè   eki   -   I went to market
     Ò   dà   udi   -   He drank

Another morphological item for expression the past is 're' or 'nure'

75. Ọ̀   dà   udi   rè   (He has drunk)
     Ọ̀   da   udi   nurè   (He has finished drinking)

The future tense

The morpheme (*cha/che*) meaning shall/ will is used to signal the future tense in addition to tonal modification. Thus we have:

76. Ọ̇   chȧ   riė   emu   (He will/wants to eat)
     Ayị chȧ   dȧ   udi   (They want to/will drink)
     Mị   chė   kpȯ   (I will/want to go home)

Apart from being used to show different tenses, tone is also used to signal negation and interrogation. For negation for example the sentence is marked with a high tone at the final syllable which too is prolonged. Consider for example:

77. Ọ̇   kpė   eki   -   She/He/It went to market
     Ọ̇   kpė   eki   -   She/He/It did not go to market

In the case of interrogation the concluding of final verb ends with a rise followed by a fall. Examples are:

78. Diė   wọ   tȧ   -   What are you talking?
     Diė   wọ̇ê   ria   -   What are you eating?

Adverbs

These are words that modify verbs, adjectives or even other adverbs. Two examples that readily come to mind are '*gangan*' and '*mamo*'. They both synonymously mean 'very well/very much'.
Examples are:

79. Okoro *hwe* Onotu   *gangan/mamo*
     i.e. 'Okoro beat Onotu very well/much'

Here the adverb *mamo* or *gangan* is used to modify the verb '*hwe*' 'beat' The same adverb can be used to modify an adjective as in

80. Uwevwi na   vwa   rhuarho mamo/gangan
     house   the   be + pres   big   very well
     i.e.   'The house is very big.'

Like adjectives, most adverbs are a product of morphological reduplication Examples are:

81.   *kpatakpata*   -   quickly

vwevwere	-	quickly
dẹnde	-	carefully
ememerha	-	carefully / gently
nanana(na)	-	now

Ideophones are also commonly used to modify verbs; i.e., they function as adverbs in the language.

82. Examples are:

Ọ   vwẹ   obọ   vwiẹ   ẹche   kọkọkọ
(He knocked at the door 'kọkọkọ' – sound of the knocking itself)

O   she   vwiẹ   ame   tefue
He fell into the water *tefue*

| *Ukokodia   na* | *sheri* | *Kprọdi* | - | The coconut fall *kprodi* |
| *Arhuaran   na* | *mudia* | *gidigba* | - | The giant stood *gidigba* |

Prepositions are used to show the relationship of one entity (animate or inanimate) to the other.

However, prepositions in Urhobo are syntactically determined. This is to say that it is their role in the sentence that should be considered.

Here are some prepositions in the language.

83.
	otọ	under
	enu	on (top of)
	oma	by, by the side of
	evu	inside
	kẹ	for/to
	rhe	to

They are used in the sentences, which follow:

84.
	Iyẹn	*na*	*ghwu*	*vwẹ*	*evu*	*rị*	*amị*	
	(A fly died in water)							
	Iyẹn	*na*	*evu*	*rị*		*amị*		(The fly is inside water)
	Iyẹn	*enu*	*ri*	*imẹjẹ*				(A fly is on a table)
	Iyen	*otọ*	*ri*	*imeje*				(A fly is under a table)
	Ọ	*viẹ*	*kẹ*	*vwẹ*				(He/She/It cried *to* me)
	O	*ru*	*kẹ*	*vwẹ*				(He/She/It did *for* me)
	O	*siẹ*	*ẹbi*	*rhe*	*vwe*			(He/She/It wrote *to* me)
	O	*siẹ*	*ẹbị*	*kẹ*	*vwẹ*			(He/She/It wrote *for* me)
	Ọmọ	*na*	*shẹ*	*kẹ*	*vwẹ*			(The child sold for/to me)

Conjunctions

These are employed in the Urhobo language to link two nominal or verbal constructions. Conjunctions in the language include such words as:

85. vẹ   -   and
    kugbe   -   and
    ti .... ti... both and
    yẹrẹ   -   or (either ... or)
    ekevuọvo   -   but

They are used in the sentences, which follow:

86. Ọmọte vẹ ọmọsharị kpệ eki (A boy and a girl went to market))
    Okọro kugbe Urȯko rhėre (Okoro and Uroko came)
    Tė Okoro tu uroko rhėre (Both Okoro and Uroko came)
    Okȯro yệrệ urȯko sȧrhe (Either Okoro or uroko can come)
    Orhere ekevuọvo o vwe rhe (He came but he is asleep)

Exclamations

Moments of surprises or sudden happenings elicit peculiar words and expressions. Some of such expressions are:

87. UU – A sound made (usually at the top of one's voice) to draw attention to incidents of fainting or fire outbreak. It is also used to show disapproval (i.e. hooting) of a neighbour's behaviour or utterance.
Ghwėkė – for drawing attention to fainting and fighting. It is also used to draw attention to incidents of lying, i.e. tell lies.
Ghwọ, Ghwo – To signal incidents of helplessness
U̇ – Used to call somebody for away, especially when there is no wish to mention the person's name.
He – This is used to draw a person's attention to oneself
Hïi – it is used to express a surprise.
Heu̇ – it is used to express disappointment. Hissing also serves the same purpose in the language.
Hu̇hu̇-Ewewu – This is used like English (Hip! Hip! Hurray!) to express jubilation.
Hi-iye: – This also is used to express jubilation.
U̇U̇-u̇ – A nasal sound made to show that one is eating something (roasted fish or meat for example) that is really delicious.

Ủ Ủ	–	This is a prolonged nasal sound made in reaction to an odour (e.g. farting or rotten food) around.
Tufię		The sound '*tufie*' often follows the one above. It is the ejection of spittle as a reaction to the abominable odour.
Nyai	–	This is a vocal reaction to something unsightly e.g. shit.
Shuọ or Shuo	–	A sound made as a sign of surprise at anything odd.
Odiómuwe		An instinctive expression of denial as when a lie is told against one.
Ọghwefịa	–	This a sound made to wish away the bad effects of anything suspected to be witchcraft.

Works cited

Holliday M. A. K., "Note on Transitivity and Theme in English Part 1," *Journal of Linguistics*, Vol.3 No.1 1967.

Stockwel *et al.*, *The Major Syntactic Structures of English*, Holt, Rinehart and Winston, 1973.

Stray P. M. H., *Modern English Structure*, Edward Arnold Ltd. London, 1962

Welmers W.C., Structural Notes on Urhobo, *JWAL* vo1, 1969.

4

Code-mixing: an investigation of English and Urhobo

– Karoh Ativie

Introduction

This essay attempts an investigation of code-mixing as it occurs in the Urhobo language. Code-mixing involves the mixing of lexical items at word level and often occurs in a multilingual country like Nigeria where several speech communities exist side by side. This phenomenon is common among most educated Nigerians and the Urhobo people who move from one code to another during conversation with such ease that it appears as if they are speaking a new and different language - a new code formed from the combination of two languages. Code-mixing is a result of language contact and shows how much languages influence each other. Code-mixing is not random as wrongly assumed but a patterned activity as this research will show. This essay acknowledges the fact that code-mixing is rule-governed and that transitions occur at specific places in sentences. In the course of this research, the following questions will be addressed:
- Who code-mixes?
- What are the reasons for code-mixing?
- When do people code-mix?
- Where in sentences do these transitions take place?

The Urhobo language

The English language is a world language spoken in many countries of the world. Urhobo, on the other hand, is little known outside Nigeria and requires an introduction.

Urhobo is a language spoken in Delta State in Nigeria and one of the most dominant and visible minority ethnic groups in the Niger Delta region of Nigeria. It spans across nine local government areas. Ukere (1990) states that there are twenty-two clans within the Urhobo-speaking polity. The word 'Urhobo' is often used interchangeably to refer to the language and to the people who speak the language.

Urhobo is a major language in Delta State used alongside Itsekiri, Ijaw, Isoko and Ukwuani languages. It is an official language in Delta State used as a medium of instruction in primary schools and in the state's television and radio stations as a means of disseminating information through public paid announcement and news-translations. It is also used alongside English in formal gatherings, churches and politics.

The Urhobo's first contact with the British came in the form of missionaries who built churches, schools, hospitals through which they established the British system of government. The English language became the language of government and, as time went on, many Urhobo had to learn English. Consequently, many Nigerians, including Urhobo, become bilinguals speaking their native language and English. Code-mixing is a result of this language contact due to the fact that when two languages exist side by side, they colour each other. Code-mixing is a notable phenomenon in the every day speech of most educated Nigerians who think in English and then express themselves in their native language.

Languages in contact

When languages come in contact, they influence each other in a number of ways. These include borrowing, code-switching and code-mixing. Borrowing involves the introduction of single words or phrases form one language to another. It is restricted to lexical items and is sometimes triggered by a lack of knowledge of the vocabulary of a language. People also borrow words from one language to express a concept or describe an object for which there is no obvious word available in the language they are using. Examples of words borrowed from English into Urhobo language are:

Urhobo	English
Ibaibol	Bible
Itelẹvishọni	Television
Itomatosi	Tomato
Itọshi	Torch

Code-switching refers to language alternation across sentence boundaries. During code-switching, the speaker changes from one language to another in the course of the conversation. The sentence below illustrates this phenomenon.

"...It is gratifying to note that a solid foundation has already been laid. *Obo avwáre guono entine* is patience, perseverance and a positive attitude. *Misieguare.*'

Kamwangalnlu (1989) defines code-mixing as language alteration within sentence boundaries. According to Akindele and Adegbite (1999), code mixing refers to a situation whereby two languages are used in a single sentence within major and minor constituent boundaries. Another example is:

Mi laiki isha-a   -   I don't like beans.

The phenomenon is also found in other parts of the world. Apple and Muysken (1987) are of the view that most of the early code-mixing studies drew on Spanish-English data recorded from conversations of Mexican Americans.

The grammar of code-mixing in Urhobo

As mentioned earlier, code-mixing is a sociolinguistics phenomenon with its own set of rules and features. In this section, we shall consider the grammar of code-mixing and then discuss the people who code-mix, when they mix, and why they mix.

Code-mixing is a rule governed activity with a grammar of its own since the result of code-mixing is language. This section attempts to investigate the grammar of code-mixing in English /Urhobo sentences.

From syntactic, evidence, it is clear that mixing is only possible in some contexts alone. First it seems that major and minor grammatical constituents may be code-mixed with Urhobo sentences. Consider the following sentences.

1. From now on, *mi gbe guọnọ we mre etine-e* - From now on, I don't want to see you here.

2. *Mi laiki isha-a* - I don't like beans

3. *Mi ka tọlọreti ri indiscipline* - I will not tolerate indiscipline

4. *Orẹyẹ ebe ri weekendi na yara.* -   He has taken the weekend papers away.

5. Honestly, *mi chese ruẹ obo wo guọnọ ni mí ru* - Honestly, I cannot do what you want me to do

6. *Yarhe, anabo tota na* in detail - Come, let us discuss the matter in detail

In 1, it is the prepositional phrase, which is inserted into the sentence. In 2, it is the verb which is mixed with the rest of the Urhobo sentence. Note that the verb has undergone a change in spelling in order to be assimilated into Urhobo. In 3, the verb and object 'tolerate' and 'indiscipline' are code-mixed. In 4, it is the word 'weekend' modifying 'papers' which is inserted. Sentences 5 and 6 show code-mixing of adjuncts in the beginning and end of sentences.

Also some of the code-mixed items may include whole phrases as in the following:

7. *Me mre re* face to face. - I saw him face to face.

8. *Aye cha* marry anytime from now.
   They will be getting married anytime from now.

Sometimes noun phrase may be code-mixed with the preceding adjectives as in 9 and 10.

9. *Mi kasa ansa're* unnecessary *kueshioni na-na.*
   I cannot answer such an unnecessary question.

10. Indecent behaviour *rowán jevwe kaka-a*
    Your indecent behaviour doesn't appeal to me at all.

Adjectives can also be inserted when they occur predicatively:

11. *Okidiagbara na selfishi mamo* - The Chairman is very selfish.

In an NP structure, English articles are not allowed in code-mixing with Urhobo. This produces ungrammatical sentences as 18 and 19 show.

12. The footprints *ore oráko.* - The footprints belong to a dog.

13. Moses *ogbe* the gate. - Moses has finished painting the gate.

The ungrammaticality of 12 and 13 is due to the fact that in Urhobo, articles come after nouns. Mixing of English pronouns in Urhobo sentence is also ungrammatical.

14. His music *vwerho vwe-e.* - His music doesn't appeal to me.

15. *She se vwi* liar. - She called me a liar.

Also ungrammatical is the repetition of the same grammatical items as in 16 and 17.

16. The woman *aye na ẹkpa*. - The woman the woman is a fool.

17. Everyday *kedekede ovwẹvwe ní mí yara*.
    Everyday he tells me to leave.

However, it is grammatical to insert the English pronoun 'you' with commands.

18. You, *huhu eche na* - You, shut the door.

The mixing of reflexive pronouns as shown in 19 is also acceptable.

19. *Vwe ne mí tetine* myself - Tell him I came here myself.

Most Urhobo are also fond of inserting English verbs into Urhobo sentence as examples 20-25 show.

20. *No sa kontrolu roye?* - Can you control him?

21. *Mí packi rí ekuakua mé* - I have packed my belongings.

22. *Mí understandi wẹ kakaka-a* - I don't understand you at all.

23. *Mí heti re oka ruemu nana.* - I hate this kind of behaviour.

24. *Die soro wo kosi re konfushion?* - Why are you causing confusion?

25. *Wane wo ka slapu mé?* - Did you say you will slap me?

Adverbs, prepositional phrases and some conjunctions may also be inserted as in the following:

26. Actually, *oshare na gbe ka rọvwọ* - Actually, the man will not marry her.

27. *Mí ka de sabato na* in a month's time. - I will buy those shoes in a month's time.

28. *Mí cha ra boti oke na jite-e.* - I will go but it's not yet time to do so.

In 26 it is the insertion of an adverb. In 27, the prepositional phrase is inserted while in 28 has English conjunctions mixed with Urhobo sentences.

As part of the grammar of code-mixing English items code-mixed with Urhobo sentences either begin or end with vowel sounds due to the fact that most nouns and adjectives in Urhobo begin or end with vowel sounds while most verbs and conjunctions end with vowel sounds. This rule applies to English words when mixed with Urhobo sentences. Let us consider the following sentences:

29. *Vue Ibroda we ne mi cha mrẹ none*
    Tell your brother that I will see him today

30. *Wo vwi problemu.* - You have problem.

31. *Mí sọpraizi nẹ ọsa tẹ ota tiọye-e*
    That she can say a thing like that does not surprise me.

32. *Ota na siriosi mamọ* - This is a serious matter.

From evidence shown, it is obvious that only certain parts of the sentence can be code-mixed. These include noun phrases, verb phrases, prepositional phrases, adverb, and conjunctions. Also we established that code-mixing avoids repetition of lexical items and the use of English articles and pronouns.

Code-mixing is not a random phenomenon. It follows certain rules and is bound by certain grammatical constraints.

Code-mixing as a sociolinguistic phenomenon

In this section, the following questions will be considered: who code-mixes? When and why they mix?

Code-mixing generally is common amongst bilinguals who move from one code to another. In the case of Urhobo, code-mixing usually occurs among Urhobo people who have identical backgrounds, who live or work in the same environment or belong to the same social circle. These include civil servants, teachers, businessmen and women and even people who know and speak little English. Among the not-so-educated, code-mixing is a means of raising their status and a way of showing that they belong to the elite class. Holmes (1992) states that code-mixing is a distinctive conversational style used among bilinguals, a rich additional linguistic resource available to them through which they convey affective meaning as well as information.

People code-mix in informal situations - e.g., parties, home, village and club meetings and also when discussing with friends, relatives and colleagues.

There are several reasons why people code-mix. First of all, when people cannot readily find appropriate Urhobo words for what they want to say, they quickly resort to using the English language. Code-mixing also serves as a means of providing a lexical filler in an utterance. English words can also be inserted into Urhobo sentences when the speaker is quoting someone else. It can also be used for emphasis to buttress the speaker's point and when a specific word is more semantically appropriate for a given concept.

People sometimes code-mix when they wish to convey confidentiality, anger or annoyance and when speakers wish to exclude someone from conservation. Another reason why people code-mix is when technical subjects for which there is no equivalent in Urhobo are being discussed.

Conclusion

Code-mixing is a result of language contact and a manifestation of the influence languages have on each other. Code-mixing in Urhoboland is common amongst the western-educated Urhobo and even the not-so-educated. It is a phenomenon that is widespread in Urhoboland and used in informal situations at home, parties, villages and club meetings and even amongst colleagues at work.

The future of code-mixing in Urhobo is uncertain. According to Essien (1995) code-mixing is like "pidginization" in several ways. Both involve the presence of a dominant language, a deviation from a 'standard' language and a mixture of more than one language. Also the grammars of both are determined by the local language (Urhobo in this case). While a pidgin may eventually become a recognized language, a code-mixed language does not. In addition, code-mixing does not necessarily require competence in either Urhobo or English language and code-mixers are often said to know neither language well. As shown in the previous section, code-mixing also depends on social and contextual factors. It may be allowed in certain situations and frowned upon in others. This attitude may reduce the practice and cause it to fade out eventually.

In conclusion, code-mixing has social, linguistic and psychological dimensions which should be further investigated, as this work is by no means exhaustive.

Works cited

Akindele, F. and Adegbite, W., *The Sociology and Politics of English in Nigeria: An Introduction*, Nigeria, Obafemi Awolowo University Press, 1999.
Apple, R. and Muysken, P., *Language Contract and Bilingualism*, London: Edward Arnold: 1987.
Essien, O., 'The English language and Code-mixing. A Case Study of the Phenomenon in Ibibio' in Bamgbose, A. *et al.* (eds), *New Englishes*: *A West African Perspective* Ibadan: Mosuro Publishers, 1995.
Ukere, A .O., *Urhobo-English Dictionary*, 1990.

Holmes, J., *An Introduction to Sociolinguistics*, London: Longman. 1992.
Kamwangamalu, N. M.. 'Languages in Contact' in Webb, V. and Kembo-Sure (eds.) *African Voices. An Introduction to the Languages and Linguistics of African*, South Africa, Oxford University Press 2000.

5

An overview of the sound system of Urhobo

– Rose Aziza

Introduction

Language, being a very important and fundamental part of human behaviour, and its nature and structure are worth studying. Language is basically speech and the spoken language is the primary form of language. This does not mean that the written language is less important. Writing is extremely important in any modern society and the more so in education. However, it must be remembered that all writing systems are based on sound systems and they attempt to depict that sound system by means of a written code. Thus, for any language to be adequately written, its sound system must be thoroughly studied and described.

Every language has a clearly distinguishable pattern of sounds. This means that each language has a set of sounds, which are combined and distributed in a particular way that makes one language different from others. Languages may share some sounds in common but the arrangement of these sounds to form words is always different. Let us consider a few examples below:

1)	**English**		**Urhobo**	
a)	sit	'sit'	se	'read, call'
b)	teik	'take'	ta	'speak, say'
c)	reinz	'rains'	ro	'grow'
d)	ləʊ	'low'	lɔ	'grind'
e)	nəʊ	'no'	nɔ	'grind'
f)	streit	'straight'	-	

In the examples in 1 above, it is obvious that the initial consonant /s, t, r, l, n/occur in both English and Urhobo and are used to form meaningful and acceptable words in the languages, but they pattern differently. In 1 (a – c), the sounds /s, t, r/ are initial consonants of words in both languages, but while in English, consonants can also end words, all Urhobo syllables are open-ended, i.e., they end with vowels.

A second difference is illustrated in 1d – e. Whereas in English /l, n/ are different *phonemes* (i.e. contrastive sounds) and so can distinguish word meaning, in Urhobo they are *allophones* (i.e. variants of the same sound) and can be used interchangeably in words because they do not distinguish word meaning.

A third difference is illustrated in 1(f), which shows an English word which begins with three consonant sounds that follow each other. This kind of combination is not permitted in the sound patterns of Urhobo, which mainly admits CV (consonant + vowel) syllables.

From the above, it is clear that each language has a systematic way in which it arranges its sounds and behind each arrangement, there is a pattern allowing or prohibiting certain sound combinations and distributions. However, for us to be able to describe a language effectively and write it down adequately, we must know what sounds are available in it and how they pattern. That two languages are so closely related that there is some degree of mutual intelligibility between them does not mean that they consistently share all sounds and the patterning of these sounds in common.

In this chapter, we shall present an outline of the sounds system of Urhobo, i.e., its consonant and vowel sound segments and how they pattern.[1] It is important to note that there are two types of phonation that are linguistically significant in Urhobo, namely, the voiced and the voiceless. Whereas all vowels, nasals, approximants and the tap are voiced, obstruents, (i.e. plosives and fricatives) are either voiced or voiceless. In the consonant chart in Table I below, the sound on the left in each box is voiceless while that on the right is voiced. In the examples that follow in sections 2 and 3, we shall show the phonemic transcriptions in slants, the phonetic transcriptions in square brackets, the orthographic representation of the words and their English equivalents.

Consonant segments

Urhobo consonant segments are presented in the chart below:

Table 1: Consonant chart for Urhobo place of articulation

Manner of Articulation	Place of articulation						
	Bilabial	Labio Dental	Alveolar	Palato Aleolar	Palatal	Velar	Labial Velar
Plosive	p b		t d		c ɟ	k g	kp gb
Fricative	ɸ	f v	s z	ʃ ʒ		h ɣ	

---

[1] For a fuller discussion, see Elugbe 1989 and Aziza 1997.

An overview of the sound system of Urhobo

Manner of Articulation	Place of articulation						
	Bilabial	Labio Dental	Alveolar	Palato Aleolar	Palatal	Velar	Labial Velar
Nasal	m		N		ɲ		ŋm
Trill			R				
Tap			ɾ				
Appro.		ʋ			j		w

(Note: Appro. = Approximant)

The chart above shows that Urhobo has twenty-eight consonant sounds. We shall now discuss each group.

Plosives

Urhobo has ten plosive segments. Plosives are consonants produced with a complete obstruction of the airstream and released with a kind of plosion. The plosive segments of Urhobo are /p, b, t, d, c, ɟ, k, g, kp, gb/

/p/ voiceless bilabial plosive, spelt in the orthography as 'p'
/pane/ - [pane] – pànè 'peel lightly'
/upe/ - [upe] – upē 'scar'
/apiapia/ - [apjapja] – ápiàpiá 'a type of bird'

/b/ voiced bilabial plosive spelt as 'b'
/bane/ - [bane] – bànè 'splash'
/obɔ/ - [obɔ] – òbọ 'hand'
/ubibɛ/ - [ubibɛ] – ubibẹ 'nail'

/t/ voiceless alveolar plosive spelt as 't'
/ta/ - [ta] – tà 'speak, say'
/otu/ - [otu] – òtù 'age group'
/utita/ - [utita] – ùtìtà 'onion'

/d/ voiced alveolar plosive spelt as 'd'
/da/ - [da] – dà 'drink'
/udi/ - [udi] – ùdì 'a drink'
/udidɛ/ - [udidɛ] – údìdẹ 'earthworm'

/c/ voiceless palatal plosive spelt as 'ch'
/co/ - [co] - chò 'steal'
/ocɛ/ - [ocɛ] - òchẹ 'water pot'
/acica/ - [acica] - àchichà 'umbrella'

/ɟ/ voiced palatal plosive spelt as 'dj'
/ɟɛ/ - [ɟɛ] - djẹ 'run'
/oɟa/ - [oɟa] - òdjà 'soap'
/aɟuɟu/ - [aɟuɟu] - àdjúdjú 'hand fan'

/k/ voiceless velar plosive spelt as 'k'
/ka/ - [ka] - kà 'stop (e.g. rain)'
/oka/ - [oka] - okà 'type'
/ukoko/ - [ukoko] - úkókō 'association'

/g/ voiced velar plosive spelt as 'g'
/ga/ - [ga] - gà 'worship, serve'
/ǫgǫ/ - [ǫgǫ] - ǫgǫ 'in-law'
/ogaga/ - [ogaga] - ògàgà 'tripod'

/kp/ voiceless labial – velar plosive spelt as 'kp'
/kpa/ - [kpa] - kpà 'vomit'
//ukpe/ - [ukpe] - úkpè 'bed'
/ukpokpo/ - [ukpokpo] - úkpòkpò 'missile'

/gb/ voiced labial –velar plosive spelt as 'gb'
/gbe/ - [gbe] - gbè 'dance'
/ogba/ - [ogba] - ógbā 'fence'
/ugbeja/ - [ugbeja] - ùgbèyán 'friend'

Fricatives

Fricatives are consonant sounds produced with a partial obstruction of the airstream. Urhobo has nine fricative consonants as described below:

/ɸ/ voiceless bilabial fricative spelt as 'ph'
/ɸo/ - [ɸo] - phò 'jump'
/uɸo/ - [uɸo] - ùphó 'throat'
/uɸɛɸɛ/ - [uɸɛɸɛ] - úphẹphẹ 'courtyard'

/f/ voiceless labiodental fricative spelt as 'f'
/fi/   -   [fi]   -   fi   'throw gift'
/ufi/   -   [ufi]   -   úfī   'rope'
/ofefe/ -   [ofefe]   -   òféfè   'emptiness'

/v/ voiced labiodental fricative spelt as 'v'
/vo/   -   [vo]   -   vò   'fetch (e.g. water)'
/uvo/   -   [uvo]   -   ùvò   'sun/sunshine'
/ovie/ -   [ovie]   -   òviè   'king'

/s/ voiceless alveolar fricative spelt as 's'
/se/   -   [se]   -   sè   'read, call'
/usi/   -   [usi]   -   ùsí   'starch'
/isiesi/ -   [isiesi] -   ísiési   'argument'

/z/ voiced alveolar fricative spelt as 'z'
/ze/   -   [ze]   -   zè   'appease'
/uzo/   -   [uzo]   -   úzò   'antelope'
/oze/   -   [oze]   -   òzé   'basin'

/ʃ/ voiceless palato-alveolar fricative spelt as 'sh'
/ʃe/   -   [ʃe]   -   shè   'fall'
/eʃa/   -   [eʃa]   -   èshà   'grey hair'
/ɔʃare/ -   [Oʃare]   -   ɔshàrè   'man, adult male'

/ĵ / voiced palato - alveolar fricative spelt as 'j'
/ĵ /   -   [ĵ]   -   jẹ   'choose'
/uĵe/   -   [uĵe]   -   uje   'twenty'
/eĵiřo/ -   [eĵiřo]   -   Éjìró   'name'

/h/ voiceless velar fricative spelt as 'h'. It has two allophones namely, [x] and [h], which are in free variation, i.e., they can be used interchangeably.
[x] is a voiceless velar fricative
[h] is a voiceless glottal fricative
/ha/   -   [ha] / [xa]   -   hà   'play'
/ɔhɔ/   -   [ɔhɔ] / [ɔxɔ]   -   ọhọ   'chicken'
/ohuo/ -   [ohwo] / [oxwo] -   òhwó   'person'

/ġ/ voiced velar fricative spelt as 'gh'
/ ġa/   -   [ġa]   -   ghà   'forbid'
/a ġã/ -   [aġã]   -   àghán   'broom'
/aġ/   -   [aġ]   -   àghọghọ   'happiness'

Nasals

Urhobo has four nasal consonants and they are described below:
/m/   voiced bilabial nasal spelt as 'm'

/mu/	-	[mu]	–	mù	'carry'
/umi/	-	[umi]	–	ùmi	'local filter'
/ama/	-	[ama]	–	ámā	'childish'

/n/   voiced alveolar nasal spelt as 'n' and sometimes as 'l'

It will be necessary to dwell a bit more on this sound. /n/ has two variants or allophones, namely, [n] and [l] and they are sometimes in free variation. Some Urhobo native speakers have argued that we need to enter both n and l as separate sounds but a closer look shows that wherever [l] is found [n] can also found. Moreover, when loan words enter into Urhobo, all cases of [l] in the original language are realized as either [n] or [r]. [l] is only heard in the speech patterns of the educated Urhobo who make a conscious effort at overcoming the [l]/ [n] alternation that Urhobo speakers are noted for. Consider the following English words as rendered by typical Urhobo speakers.

2 a) look   – [nuk]
   b) Lagos   – [negǫsu]
   c) table   – [iteboro]
   d) school – [isikuru]

We therefore recognise /n/ as the phoneme and [l] as a variant.

/nɔ/	-	[nɔ] / [lɔ]	–	nǫ	'grind'
/une/	-	[une] /[ule]	–	une	'song'
/inekuku/	-	[inekuku]/[ilekuku]	–	inekuku	'pigeon'

/ ɲ / voiced palatal nasal spelt as 'ny'

/ɲo/	-	[ɲ o]	–	nyò	'hear'
/ɔɲa/	-	[ɲ a]	–	ǫnyā	'prawn'
/ɔɲɔ/	-	[ɔɲɔ]	–	ǫnyǫ	'honey bee'

/ ŋm/ voiced labial-velar nasal spelt as 'mw'

/ŋma/	-	[ŋma]	–	mwà	'extract (e.g. oil from palm fruit)'
/aŋma/	-	[aŋmá]	–	amwa	'cloth'
/uŋmu/	-	[ùŋmù]	–	umwu	'drug'

Rhotics

Urhobo has two rhotics as described below:

/r/ voiceless alveolar trill spelt as 'rh'
    /re/   -   [re]   –   rhè   'come'
    /ure/   -   [ure]   –   úrhe   'tree'
    /iribo/   -   [iribo]   –   irhíbó   'pepper'

/ɾ/ voiced alveolar tap spelt as 'r'. It has two allophones [ɬ] and [ɾ] which are sometimes in complementary distribution.
[ɬ] is a tapped alveolar lateral which occurs in a nasal environment

[mra]   - [mɬa] /[mra]   – mrà   'be loud (of sound)'
/orĩ/   - [orĩ] /[oɬi]   – ɔ̀rìn   'puss'
/urĩrĩ/   - [u rĩrĩ] /[uɬiɬi]   – ùrìrìn 'glory'

[ɾ] is a voiced alveolar tap found elsewhere
    /re/   –   [re]   –   rè   'eat'
    /ori/   –   [ori]   –   ɔ̀rí   'pomade'
    /erere/   –   [erere]   –   èrèrè   'profit'

Approximants

These are sounds pronounced with an open approximation of the vocal organs and have no audible friction. There are three of them in Urhobo, namely, /ʋ, j, w/ and each of them may be nasalised in the environment of a nasal vowel. Consequently, each of them has two allophonic variants as indicated below:

         [ṽ, ȷ̃, w̃] before nasal vowels
         [ʋ, j, w] before oral vowels

/ʋ/ voiced labiodental approximant spelt as 'vw'
    /ʋo/   - [ʋo]   –   vwò   'have'
    /uʋõ/   - [uṽõ]   –   úvwon   'flesh'
    /rukɛʋɛ/   - [rukɛʋɛ]   –   rúkẹvwẹ   'blessed me'

/j/ voiced palatal approximant spelt as 'y'
    /ja/   -   [ja]   –   yà   'catch'
    /ujɛ/   -   [ujɛ]   –   úyẹn   'fly'
    /aje/   -   [aje]   –   àyè   'woman'

/w/ voiced labial– velar approximant spelt as 'w'
/wã/   -   [wã]   –   wàn   'pass (by)'
/owe/ -   [owe] –   òwè   'bush mango'
/ɾukɛwɛ/ - /ɾukɛvvɛ/ -   rúkẹwẹ 'blessed you'

Vowel segments

At the phonetic level, Urhobo has seven oral vowels, namely,

Close/High	i	u
Close-mid	e	o
Open-mid	ɔ	ɛ
Open		a

These seven vowels are also those used for writing the language. However, the behaviour of the vowels /e/ and /o/ in utterances indicates that we must recognise two kinds of /e/ and /o/ respectively, thus making a total of nine vowels. Consider the behaviour of /e/ and /o/ in the following groups of words

Group 1: *Nouns*

èrhù	'cap'	ìrhu	'caps'
èránkò	'dog'	èránkò	'dogs'
òzé	'basin'	ìzé	'basins'
òtá	'word'	età	'words'

Group 2: *Verbs*

sè	'read, call'	èsé	'to read, to call'
rè	'eat'	ẹriọ [ɛrjɔ]	'to eat'
dò	'throw'	èdó	'to throw'
sò	'sing'	ẹsuọ [ɛswɔ]	'to sing'

The examples above show that /e/ and /o/ pattern differently in grammatical sequences, evidence that these vowels are the result of some kind of vowel merging. This is a common phenomenon in the vowel systems of Edoid languages which are said to have been reduced from a ten vowel system postulated for Proto – Edoid (PE) (Elugbe 1973, 1989). Although vowel reduction appears to be complete at the surface phonetic level, the vowels still retain some of their original features at the phonological level and this is responsible for the differences in their patterning when they occur in grammatical sequences. In order to make this work clearer, we shall recognise nine vowels at the phonological level but seven at the phonetic and orthographic levels as shown in Table 2.

Table 2: Urhobo vowel segments

Phonological	phonetic	orthographic
i	i	i
I		
e ⎫	e	e
ɛ ⎭	ɛ	e
a	a	a
ɔ	ɔ	ɔ
o	o	o
ǫ		
u	u	u

Each vowel segment may be inherently or phonetically nasalised and so no separate treatment will be given to nasal vowels. The morphemes below demonstrate the oral/nasal vowel contrasts in Urhobo.

Example 1:

Oral/nasal vowel contrasts

Phoneme		Pronunciation	Spelling	Gloss
/i/	/ori/ -	[ori]	òrí	'pomade'
	/orĩ/ -	[orĩ]	òrìn	'puss'
/I/	/rI/ -	[re]	rè	'eat'
	/sĨ/ -	[sẽ]	sèn	'refuse, reject'
/e/	/se/ -	[se]	sè	'read, call'
	/ʒẽ/ -	[ʒẽ]	jèn	'like'
/ɛ/	/sɛ/ -	[sɛ]	sę	'be efficacious'
	/kpɛ/ -	[kpɛ]	kpęn	'peel'
/a/	/ɣarI/ -	[ɣare]	ghàre	'divide, share'
	/ɣrI/ -	[ɣãre]	ghànre	'be expensive'
/ɔ/	/gɔ/ -	[gɔ]	gǫ	'worship'
	/vɔ/ -	[vɔ]	vǫn	'be ful l'
/o/	/fo/ -	[fo]	fò	'fit'
	/fõ/ -	[fõ]	fòn	'be clean'

/ẹ /	/sU /	-	[so]	sò	'sing'
	/fU/	-	[fõ]	tòn	'extinguish'
/u/	/ku/	-	[ku]	kù	'pour'
	/vũ /	-	[vũ]	vùn	'up roof'

Vowel sequences

Vowel sequences are highly attested within stems and across morpheme and word boundaries in Urhobo. The morphology of the language is such that nouns as well as qualifiers (adjectives, quantifiers, demonstratives and possessive pronouns) begin with a prefix of some sort and end with a vowel. The prefixes attached to nouns and qualifiers function as concord markers, which express number concord with their head nouns. Verbs, adverbs as well as auxiliaries begin with consonants but also end with vowels Thus, all Urhobo lexical items end with vowels while quite a number also begin with vowels. This means that whenever two lexical items are in sequence, they almost always make vowels available at their boundaries and there are no restrictions as to the type of vowels that may occur at morpheme boundaries.

Example 2:

Vowel sequence across morpheme boundaries

a)	fì throw	+	íghō money	
b)	rè eat	+	ọrẹ plantain	
c)	kù pour	+	ùdì drink	
d)	sò sing		ùnè song	
e)	sè read	+	ọbè book	
f)	shẹ sell	+	àmwá cloth	

g)	dò	+	ékpù
	throw		bag
h)	kọrọ	+	émámọ
	pluck		fruit
i)	sà	+	òhwó
	shoot		person

In addition to this, a number of lexical items exist which have sequences of vowels in their stems but the patterning of these vowels is restricted: the first vowel must always be a [High] or close vowel /i/ or /u/ and the second must be a non-identical vowel. Thus, the vowel sequences /ie, iẹ, ia, io, iọ, ue, uẹ, ua, uo, uọ/ can be found within morpheme stems while the sequence ii, iu, ui, uu are not permitted. Take a look at the examples in 5 below

Example 3:

                Vowel sequences within morpheme stems

a)   ò – viè   'king'

b)   ó – viẹ   'a cry'

c)   ọ - sià   'bush dog'

d)   ò – siò   'rain'

e)   rhiọ   'be early'

f)   ù – bue   'dust'

g)   ó – vuẹ   'a message'

h)   kuà   'pack'

i)   ú – suo   'administration

j)   guọ - nọ   'look for'

However, the syllable structure of Urhobo prohibits vowels sequences from occurring at the phonetic level. Therefore when these sequences occur in the underlying representation, they obligatorily undergo some systematic phonological processes to arrive at the acceptable phonetic forms and the two common processes are vowel elision (VE) or glide formation (GF).

Vowel elision
Vowel elision is a process, which fuses lexical sequences together by deleting either of two vowels occurring across a morpheme boundary. The choice of the eliding vowel is determined by the morphosyntactic relations occurring between the lexical items such that a grammatically functional vowel, e.g. a noun or qualifier prefix, which indicates number alternations, is usually retained while a grammatically vacuous vowel such as a noun or a verb stem vowel or the prefix vowel of a demonstrative is deleted. See the examples in 6 below:

6a) *émọ*   +   *ĭvẹ*   -   *émØ* + *ĭvẹ*   –   [*émivẹ*]
     children   two   'two children'

b)   *úko*   +   *ọnana*   –   *úkó* + *Ønààna*   [*úkó nànà*]
     cup   this one   'this cup'

c)   *dẹ*   +   *úkó*   –   *dØ* + *úkó*   [*dúkó*]
     buy   cup   'buy a cup'

d)   *ọmọtẹ*   +   *óyóyòvwí*   –   *ọmọtØ* + *óyóyòvwi* – [*ọmọtóyóyòvwì*]
     girl   beautiful   'beautiful girl'

e)   *émétẹ*   +   *íyóyòvwì*   –   *émétØ* + *íyóyòvwi* – [*émétíyóyòvwì*]
     girls   beautiful   'beautiful girls'

Glide formation
Glide formation is a process whereby a [+High] vowel occurring immediately before another vowel is realised as a non–syllabic glide. This means that the [+High, +Front] vowels /i/ and /I/ may each be realised as the palatal approximant [j] while the [High, Back] vowels /u/ and /U/ may each be realised as the labial – velar approximant [w] when any of them occurs as the first vowel in a sequence within or across word/morpheme boundaries. Within a morpheme boundary, the second vowel is required to be non-identical with the first, i.e. sequences such as *ii, *iu, *ui, *uu do not occur. Across a morpheme boundary the second vowel may be any vowel but it must be grammatically relevant so that it can be retained. Compare the forms in 7 with those in 8 below.

7. Glide formation within morpheme boundaries

   a) /ovie/ – [ovje] – òviè 'king'
   b) /riɔ/ – [rjɔ] – rhio 'be early'
   c) /ovuɛ/ – [ovwɛ] – óvue 'a message'
   d) /kua/ – [kwa] – kuà 'pack'

8. Glide formation across morpheme boundary

   a) /fi iɣo/ –[fjiɣo] – fì íghō 'throw money'
   b) /rI ɔrɛ/– [rjɔrɛ]– rè orhẹ 'eat plantain'
   c) /ku udi/ – [kwudi] – kù ùìdi 'pour drink'
   d) /sU une/ – [swune] – sò ùène 'sing a song'

Both vowel elision and glide formation are complementary processes which are boundary eliminating; they turn two syllables in underlying representation into one in the phonetic realization. This means that in a fairly long utterance a number of vowels may either be elided or become non-syllabic glides but adequate provision is made for the listener to facilitate his interpretation of the phonetic string.

Vowel harmony[2]

Vowel harmony in a process whereby the vowels of a given language can be divided into two mutually exclusive sets such that the vowels of a given morpheme, word or verbal phrase are selected from any one of the two sets. The vowel in each set can co-occur with themselves to the exclusion of the vowels of the other set. The phenomenon is attested in many Niger-Congo languages. In the Edoid languages, PE ten vowels are divided into the two groups in 9 below on the basis of tongue height. The term used is Advanced Tongue Root (ATR).

9. Set I [+ATR]   Set 2 [- ATR]
   i   u   I   U
   e   o   ɛ   ɔ
       ə   a

It must be noted that only Degema, a Delta Edoid language of Rivers State, still retains all the ten vowels of PE in its vowel inventory. Most others have reduced theirs to eight or seven as a result of vowel merging and the pattern of reduction, according to Elugbe (1989: 119) is one of the following:

---

[2] For a fuller discussion of Vowel Harmony in Urhobo, see Aziza (1994. 1997).

(a) In the nine vowel systems, there is no /ə/
(b) In the eight vowel systems, there are no /ə/, /I/
(c) In the seven vowel system, there are no /ə/, /I/, and /U/

Urhobo is an example of the last possibility, as it has only seven vowels. There is evidence to show that PE */ə/ has merged with/ɛ/ in words like [ukɛ] 'egg', [utiɛ], 'Orange'; that /I/ has merged with /e/ in words like /sẽ/ 'reject, [ɔke] 'time as well as the prefix vowel /e/ found with [- ATR] nouns and verbs; that *U has merged with/o/ in words like [ɔso] 'hawk', [odɛ], name. Vowel merging is what has led to there being two types of /e/ and/ o/ in Urhobo i.e. they sometimes behave as high vowels when they are actually PE [+ATR] */I/ and */U/ and sometimes as low vowels where they are actually [+ATR] /e/ and /o/.

Vowel harmony exists in varying degrees in noun and verbal constructions in Urhobo. The phenomenon is root controlled in this language such that the stem vowel controls the type of affixes it takes. This means that affixes must agreed in [ATR] with the stem vowels: if the stem vowel is [+ATR], the affixes are [+ATR] and if the stem vowel is [- ATR], the affixes would also surface as [- ATR].

However as a result of vowel merging mentioned above, the ten vowels of Proto Edoid has been reduced to seven in Urhobo and as such the language operates what is called partial vowel harmony. For this reason, two seemingly identical morphemes may behave differently when they appear in certain constructions. Examine the forms in 10 and their behaviour in the sequences in 11 and 12 below.

10. (a) sè   –   [se]   'call, read'
    (b) dò   –   [do]   'throw'
    (c) rè   –   [re]   'eat'
    (d) sò   –   [so]   'sing'

In the infinitive, these verbs pattern as in 9 below

11. (a) èsé   –   [ese]   –   ese   'to call, to read'
    (b) èdó   –   [edo]   –   edo   'to throw'
    (c) ẹriọ –   [ɛrjɔ] –   ẹriọ   'to eat'
    (d) ẹsuọ –   [ɛswɔ] –   ẹsuọ   'to sing'

In a verbal construction they also take different pronouns

12. (a) ò sé ọbè – [o sɔbe] 'he read a book'
    (b) ò dó úkó – [o duko] 'he threw a cup'
    (c) ọ ré ọnẹ – [ɔ rjɔnɛ] 'he ate yam'
    (d) ọ só ùnè – [ɔ swune] 'he sang a song'

Vowel harmony in the noun

A noun in Urhobo is generally made up of a prefix vowel and a stem, which consists of at least a consonant and one or two vowel segments. Vowel harmony is less apparent in the noun class than in the verb class mainly due to vowel merging. However it manifests itself very clearly in the way nouns in Urhobo form their plurals. This is done by alternating the prefix vowel of the singular noun with another vowel and it is the stem vowel that determines this alternation. If the noun stem vowel is [+ATR], the plural prefix would be /i/ but if it is [-ATR], the plural prefix would be /e/. Examples are in 13 and 14 below

13. [+ATR] stem Vowels
    a) ìdjérhè   'a road'   ìdjérhè 'roads'
    b) ùdì   ' a drink'   ìdì   'drinks'
    c) ébò   'a sack'   íbò   'sacks'
    d) odō   'a mortar'   idō   'mortars'

14. [- ATR] stem vowels
    a) èrankò   'a dog'   èrankò   'dogs'
    b) òde   'a name'   èdẹ   'names'
    c) ọbò   'a doctor'   èbò   'doctors'
    d) àghán   'a broom'   èghán   'brooms'

There is also a group of nouns which Elugbe (1973) referred to as 'paired body parts. These form their plural by alternating the singular prefix vowel with /a/ instead of /i/ or /e/ as indicated in 15 below:

15. Paired body parts
    a) òwọ   'a leg'   àwọ   'legs'
    b) òbo   ' a hand'   àbọ   'hands'
    c) ẹrò   'eyer'   àrò   'eyes'
    d) àkòn   'tooth'   àkòn   'teeth'

Vowel harmony in the verbal system

Vowel harmony is particularly apparent in the verbal system of Urhobo. The vowels of affixes which accompany verb stems, such as, subject and object pronouns, concord markers, tense/aspect markers are required to agree in [ATR] harmony with the verb stem vowel(s). The examples in 16 - 19 below explain this point clearly.

16. The infinitive/gerundive

Verb stem   **Infinitive/gerund**

a) /si/ – [si]   sì 'write' = /esio/ – [esjo] èsió 'to write, (act of writing)'
b) /rɪ/ – [rɛ]   rè 'eat' = /ɛrɪɔ/– [ɛrjɔ] ẹrio 'to eat, (act of eating),
c) /se/ – [se]   sè 'read' = /ese/– [ese] èse 'to read, (act of reading)'
d) /ku/ – [ku]   kù 'pour' = /ekuo/–[ekwo] ekuó 'to pour, (act of pouring)'
e) /sU/ – [so]   sò 'sing' = /ɛsʊɔ/– [ɛswɔ] ẹsuọ 'to sing, (act of singing)'
f) /do/ – [do]   dò 'throw' = /edo/– [edo] èdó 'to throw, (act of throwing)'
g) /da/ – [da]   da 'drink' = /ɛ da/– [ɛda] ẹda 'to drink, (act of drinking'

17. Pronoun + verb

    a)   mì   sírìi   'I wrote'
    b)   mì   kúrù   'I poured';
    c)   mì   séri   'I read'
    d)   mè   rérè   'I ate'
    e)   mè   sórò   'I sang'
    f)   mè   dárè   'I drank'

18. Pronoun + verb + pronoun

    a)   ò   mú   vwé   'He carried me'
    b)   mì   sé   wé   'I called you'
    c)   wo   sì   ró   'You wrote it'
    d)   mè   ré   rọ   'I ate it'
    e)   wọ   só   vwẹ   'You sang me'
    f)   ọ   dá   rọ   'He drank it'

19. Future tense

    a)   mì   chè   sé   'I will call (him)'
    b)   ó   chè   kuó   'He will pour (it)'
    c)   wó   chè   sió   'You will write (it)'
    d)   ọ   chà   suọ   'He will sing (it)'
    e)   mé   chà   riọ   'I will eat (it)'
    f)   wọ   chà   dá   'You will drink (it)'

Syllable structure

So far, we have been discussing the segments that make up speech in Urhobo and their behaviour. From our discussion so far, it is clear that the flow of speech can be divided up into segments and that segments are characterized by phonetic properties which can interact with each other. We shall conclude this chapter with a brief examination of the syllable structure.

The syllable is at the heart of phonological representation. It is a unit in terms of which phonological systems are organised. It is a purely phonological entity which cannot be identified with a grammatical or semantic unit. This is because a grammatical word may consist of one, two or more syllables. The syllable has its own internal structure, consisting of an ONSET (which comes at the beginning) and a RHYME (which follows it). The rhyme may in turn consist of the NUCLEUS (i.e. the syllable core) and the CODA. Thus, the structure of a syllable may be represented as in 20 below:

20.

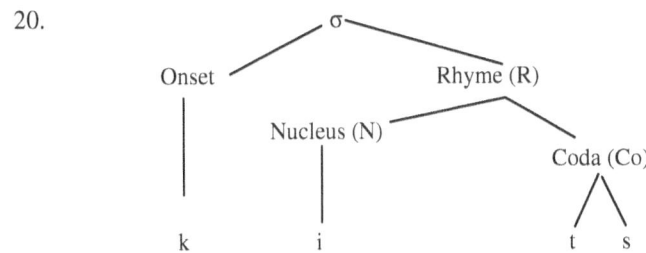

Internal structure of the English word 'kits'

Both the onset and the coda consist of consonant segments while the nucleus consists of syllabic segments, i.e. a vowel or a syllabic consonant. The nucleus is the only obligatory member of the syllable. Consequently, a syllable may be made up of only the nucleus, usually a vowel and one or more consonants before and/or after the vowel - e.g.

21. (a) (Urhobo) [e] 'yes' - only V
    (b) (Urhobo) [da] 'drinks' - CV
    (c) (English) [bred] 'bread' - CCVC
    (d) (English) [sprint] 'sprint' - CCCVCC

At the phonological level, Urhobo syllable structure can be summarised as follows:

22.

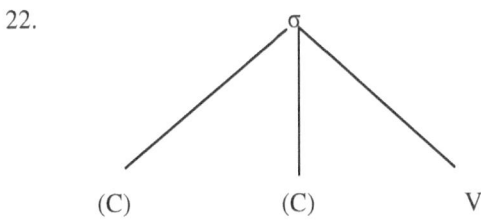

Where σ stands for the syllable, (C) for optional consonant segments and V for the obligatory vowel segment. There are no syllabic consonants. Urhobo operates a rule of syllabification that inserts a syllable boundary after each vowel segment. We thus have a situation where all the syllables are open. The following syllable structures are possible in Urhobo.

23. (a) V
     (a) CV
     (b) CCV

The V syllable

The V syllable consists of a vowel as the only segment; it is the minimum syllable type in Urhobo. It can occur as a word or initially in a phonological word such as in nouns, adjectives, and demonstratives, as well as in the formation of the gerundive and the infinitive forms of verbs, as a prefix of some sort. Examples:

24. a) è   V   interjection   'denotes a positive response'
     b) ò ~ǫ   V   Pronoun.   '3rd person singular'
     c) u – kpè   V– CV   noun   'bed'
     d) o-nà-nà   V-CV-CV   demonstrative   'this (one)'
     e) ǫ-gá-gàn   V-CV-CV   adjective   'strong'

The CV syllable

The CV syllable consists of a consonant element C and the nucleus V. It is the predominant syllable structure in the language. It can occur as a word or in the initial, medial of final position in the phonological word.

25. (a) sà   CV   Verb   'shoot'
     (b) gbè   CV   Verb   'dance'
     (c) kpò-kpò   CV-CV   Verb   'Worry'
     (d) èrhù   V – CV   Noun   'Cap/hat'
     (e) kpà-tà-kpà-tà   CV-CV-CV-CV   Adverb   'hurriedly'

The CCV syllable

This syllable type consists of two marginal consonant elements, C_1 and C_2 and the obligatory V element. It can also occur as a word or in any position in a word. However, there are collocational restrictions on the type of consonant segments found in this syllable. At the phonological level, the first consonant must be either a labial or velar consonant while the second consonant must be the voiced alveolar tap /r/. Examples:

26. (a)   brù   CCV   Verb   'cut

(b)	hrà	CCV	Verb		'scatter'
(c)	ò-gbrù	V-CCV	Noun		'male garment'
(d)	à - phrò	V-CCV	Noun	'argument'	
(e)	ìi-brè-hè	V-CCV-CV	Noun	'mud'	

However, at the phonetic level as a result of the application of glide formation rules, three types consonants are permitted in C_2 position, namely [rẹ], [j] and [w]. As discussed in section 3 above, the application of glide formation rules necessitates the application of the principle of re-syllabification since all Urhobo syllables must end with a vowel. Therefore, the second syllable, which consists of only a vowel segment ceases to be a syllable and is annexed to the first syllable in order to provide the obligatory nucleus to make the syllable complete. This means that what was underlyingly a sequence of two syllables, CV-V, gets realised as a single syllable with a consonant cluster [CCV] in which C_2 is either [j] or [w]. Examples are in 27 below:

27. (a) mì – è   CV – V   = [mje]   CCV   'take'
    (b) ò – sì – ò   V – CV – V   = [osjo] VCCV   'rain'
    (c) ú – tí -ẹn   V – CV – V   = [utjɛ] VCCV   'orange'
    (d) sì + ọ - bè   CV + V – CV   = [sjɔbe] CCVCV   'write a book'
    (e) gù – à   CV – V   = [gwa]   CCV   'drive'
    (f) è – mú-o   V – CV – V   = [emwo] VCCV   'to carry'
    (g) kù+ì–rhi-bó CV + V – CV – CV = [kwiribo] CCVCVCV 'pour pepper'
    (h) dà + ù – dì   CV + V-CV   = [dudi] CVCV   'take a drink'
    (i) sè + ọ- bè   CV + V – CV   = [sɔbe] CVCV   'read a book'

The examples in 27 (h) and (i) show that where vowels are elided, re-syllabification also takes place so that an original CV + V syllable sequence is realised as simply CV.

Conclusion

We have discussed some of the characteristics of the sound system of Urhobo. We hope sincerely that we have been able to clarify a few thorny points that can help us write Urhobo better. Since writing derives from speech, there can be no proper writing system without an adequate description of the sound system of the language. Although most of the subject matter addressed here has been scantily treated because of the scope of the work, it is hoped that it has provided a good beginning and a better understanding of how the Urhobo language works.

Selected references

Aziza, R. O., 'Vowel Harmony in Urhobo,' *Nigerian Language Studies* 2:1 – 7, 1994.
Aziza, R. O., 'Urhobo Tone System,' PhD thesis, University of Ibadan, 1997.
Elugbe, B. O., 'A Comparative Edo Phonology,' PhD thesis, University of Ibadan, 1973.
Elugbe, B. O., *Comparative Edoid: Phonology and Lexicon*, Delta Series No. 6, University of Port Harcourt Press. 1989
Kelly, J., 'Urhobo' in E. Dunstan (ed.) *Twelve Nigerian Languages*, London, Longman, 1969, pp. 153 – 161.

6

The Urhobo language and the challenges of modernity

– Igho J. Onose

When a people, for example the Yoruba, the Igbo, the Ijaw, are mentioned, what strikes the hearer at first is perhaps the language of the people so mentioned. This is about the most binding factor that holds them as one and makes them unique and different from any other group of peoples. This is perhaps the reason why language groups guard against the imposition of another language on them by way of political domination or military conquest, if they can. Language, apart from identifying a people as a group, is a repository of the cultural values, norms, belief system and practices of a people. "In this perspective," says G.E. Sadjere, "language becomes the most effective bank of the people's customs and traditions." One of the greatest things that can happen to a people is to rob them of their language. This situation would simply mean another "Things Fall Apart". The importance of language to a people is recognized in the social sciences as in other branches of study. Language, in the words of Otite, "constitutes a principal part of the culture and a chief means and strategy for its preservation and transmission."

In this essay an attempt is made to diachronically survey the changes in the Urhobo language since the planting of English as the official language of Nigeria. By way of introduction, "the Urhobo people," according to Otite, "now live in a territory bounded by Latitudes 6° and 5° 15[1] North and longitude 5° 40[1] and 6° 25[1]East in the Delta State of Nigeria. Their neighbours are the Isoko to the South East, the Itsekiri to the West, the Bini to the North, the Ijo to the South and the Ukwani to the North-East." It must be pointed out that the Urhobo language covering a geographical expanse of land as already hinted above and embracing many clans - twenty-two in all - is a cover term for a conglomeration of many dialects, which as dialects are mutually intelligible. The Urhobo man from Kokori in Agbon clan has a different dialect from an Urhobo man from Abraka, or Orogun or Agbarho. In spite of these differences, which are mainly accentual, indigenes of these dialect areas can discuss in Urhobo, each in his dialect, and feel satisfied that they have understood themselves well, as indeed they have.

This writer looks at the Urhobo languages from his dialect (Agbon) and assumes the lexis and structure of his dialect for the entire language. The differences among the dialects, as already said, do not preclude intelligibility. It must be recognized that outside linguistic influences apart, every language is as intrinsically alive and in 'a state of becoming' as much as its people and their practices. If this were not the case there would be a development gap between a people and their language. To avoid this situation a language must be necessarily as dynamic as its people. There is no point at which any language is static as long as it serves a people and their culture. This fact is well recognized in the literature. To Robins, "The fact of continuous, though gradual change in language at every level, phonetic, phonological, grammatical, and lexical, is indisputable; indeed, the assumption, for the purposes of description, of a stage of a language at which no change is recognized as occurring is strictly speaking in the nature of a fictional abstraction."

Two influences, namely internal and external, have often been held accountable for the change. Internally, people develop artistically and in taste as well as in other spheres of their cultural life with time. This necessitates a linguistic change. Also externally, it is impossible to always ward off the influences of the neighbouring or politically dominating people and their languages. These two factors, especially the latter, have account for the modification the Urhobo language has undergone. In course of such development says Robbins '...new products often require new designations and some words pass out of current vocabulary as the particular sorts of objects or ways of behaving to which they refer become obsolete.'

The changes in the Urhobo language are going to be reviewed and discussed against the background of the cultural development and shifts of emphasis in the practices of the people through time on the one hand, and against the impact of the adjoining languages earlier mentioned, but particularly the English language, the language of inter-tribal communication in Nigeria and many other countries of the world. Before Nigeria was colonized, and even more during the colonial era, the Urhobo, who were predominantly farmers, palm-nut collectors and trappers, were involved in commercial activities with their neighbours: the Itsekiri, the Ijaw, the Ukwani and the Bini.

These commercial activities which paved way for inter-tribal marriages among them cannot be said to have left the language without a mark. One way in which this situation betrays itself is in naming. There are a few Urhobo indigenes that have Itsekiri, Ijaw or Ukwani names. Some of the objects of commerce also came into the buying land along with their indigenous names.

The focus of this essay is, however, more, than anywhere else, on the impact of the English language on Urhobo and how the Urhobo language has survived, without being inundated and supplanted, the onslaught of the English language. One must add here that the English language itself has in course of history come under the influence of other languages, notable among which are Greek, Latin and French. It was so much that at a time the language of scholarship in England was Latin and that of the high table and etiquette was French. The English language itself was castigated as a provincial language of the untutored and ignorant peasants. Thanks to history, however, events unfolded to bring English to the world status that it enjoys today. The scars of its chequered history are discernible in the words still current in the language today. These are words which originally were Greek, Latin or French.

According to Barber, 'One result of the Latin influence on English during the Renaissance was the introduction of a large number of Latin words into the language...the peak period was between about 1550 and 1650.' It is reported that many Latin words came into the language during the Middle English period. These included religious terms like 'requiem' and 'gloria', words from the law courts like 'clients', 'executor', 'conviction' and 'memorandum', medical and scientific words like 'recipe', 'dissolve', 'distillation', 'concrete' 'comet' and 'equator' and abstract words like 'adoption' 'conflict', 'dissent', 'imaginary' and 'implication'. The saga for loaning words got more impetus with the inception of science and technology, which required terms for new concepts and discoveries. This is how such scientific terms as 'pattern', 'vacuum', equilibrium', 'momentum' and mathematical terms such as 'area', 'radius', 'series' and 'calculus' came into the language. Latin and Greek were not the only sources of loaned words. From Italian in the Renaissance period came 'madrigal' and 'opera' in music; 'sonnet' in literature; 'fresco', 'cameo' and 'relief' in visual arts; 'cornice' and 'cupola' in 'architecture'. In the area of warfare are such terms as 'squadron', 'parapet', 'salvo', and 'bandit' and in commerce are Italian loans such as 'traffic', 'contraband', 'argosy' and 'frigate'.

Britain's active participation in world trade has fetched words for the language from here and there. Thus, this has plucked such words as 'pyjamas' from India, 'bamboo' from Malaya, 'maize' from the West Indies, 'budgerigar' from Australia, 'tomato' from Mexico, 'coffee' from Turkey and 'tea' from China.

The foregoing goes to underscore the influences of contact which one language can receive from other languages. In the case of Urhobo which is the language of appraisal, one will not be surprised if loans and loaning seem to become the order of the day, especially, as the English language in home truth, is a more technologically advanced language than Urhobo. Since the fifteenth century when the English language gained a foothold on our land, a lot of changes, though in most cases imperceptible as such changes often are elsewhere, have occurred in the language. These changes as already highlighted are partially consequent on the second language and also often a part and process of the normal evolution of a language in consonance with the culture of the people. To take a very simple but important change in the language, we look at the greeting and its wording in the language. In the words of Otite evidence of changes in Urhobo language are well known. For example the Urhobo once said "*nawede*" that is "*migwo*" being a salutation meaning literally 'I kneel for you': The response was '*bromarikpekpeghe*' or '*naragha*' that is '*vredo*' meaning literally "get up, thank you".

When the whites came to Urhobo land one of their problems apart from mosquitoes was the language of communication. The Urhobo language was phonologically very different from Portuguese, Dutch or English. In addition to evolving pidgin for communication with the indigenes, the whites, among other linguistic blemishes they wrought on the language, resorted to dephonimization or reinterpretation of the basic sounds of Urhobo and consequently mispronounced long established words and names in the language. This accounts for such anglicised pronunciations as:

Abraka for the local word Avwraka
Kokori for Uhwokori
Sapele for Urhiaphele
Effurun for Evwro, and
Ughelli for Ughene

It is normal cultural evolution expedited by colonial influences that altered the numeral system of the language. As stated by Ofua 'the Urhobo ancient method or process of numbering or computing emanated from the counting of cowries that had intrinsic value of monetary worth.'(31) The counting at the time went as follows:

Ughovo	1	cowrie
Ighava	2	cowries
Igharha	3	``
Ighane	4	``
Ijorin	5	``
Ighesan	6	``
Igheghwre	7	``
Igherenren	8	``
Ighirhirin	9	``
Ighighwe	10	``
Ufi	20	``
Ogbigho	30	``
Ujorin	100	``
Ochoho	140	``
Uri	200	``
Uchaohava	280	``
Asa	440	``
Eravweavo	640	cowries

Ebo	840	``
Egwre	980	``
Ibuje	16,800	``
Igbogban	25,200	cowries

Native speakers of the language can easily tell that the system above is quite different from that adopted today, the few similarities notwithstanding. For example it can be said that such numerical terms as '*Ufi*' 20, '*Ochoho*' 140, '*Asa*' 440, '*Ebo*' 840, and '*Ibuje*' 16,800, do not exist in any morphological semblance in the language today.

The emphasis in this chapter is on what factors have accounted for the survival of Urhobo as a language today in the face of the eclipsing presence of English. Two main processes were adopted by the language in order to successfully exist along-side English. These are internal morphological processes to evolve new words for new ideas and objects. For example from the word '*hwa*' which means 'clasp' another one '*ahwa*' was formed to denote pliers. In the same way from '*hwe*' i.e. laugh '*ehwe*' meaning laughter was evolved.

The second process of word formation was borrowing loaning from English. These loans were in most cases made to conform to the morphological pattern of Urhobo words before they were fully accepted in the language. To take a simple example, the English syllable structure is C V as in tea but that of Urhobo is VC V. This is why tea in English has become '*Iti*' in Urhobo. In Urhobo, nominals tend to begin and end with a vowel sound. Therefore, any word borrowed from English, including names of people, is made to conform to this pattern. Another change is the rhythm. English has a stress-timed rhythm while Urhobo has a syllable-timed rhythm indicated orthographically with tone marks. Thus the English "brother" becomes Urhobo '*ibròda*'. In many areas of human endeavour, we find loans from English into Urhobo which have been made to conform morphologically to the Urhobo pattern. An attempt is made to enumerate some below:

In the area of religion and worship we have:

English	**Urhobo**
Church	*Ishóshi*
Rev. Father	*Ifadá*
Bible	*Ibáibolo*
Catechist	*Ikátikísti / Ikátikisi*
Pastor	*Ipásto / Ipasito*
Choir	*Ikuáya*

Communication media

Radio	*Irédio*
Television	*Itenivíshoni*
Telephone	*Itenifónu*

86 The Urhobo language today

Telegraph	*Itanigôfu*
Motor	*Imóto*
Bicycle	*Ibásíkoro*
Motorcycle	*Imótosakoro* (or recently *Imashini* or *Okada*)

Educational establishment

School	*Isukúru*
Class	*Iklási*
Teacher	*Itísha*
(Headmaster) HM	*Éshemu*
Dictionary	*Idishónári*
Ball	*Ibólo*
High jump	*Ijópu*
Register	*Irhéjísta*
Diary	*Idâri*
Ink	*Íki*

Dressing

Pants	*Ipánti*
Underwear	*Odaghwie*
Shorts/knickers	*Iníka*
Trousers	*Itróza*
Coat	*Ikótu*
Towel	*Itáwáni*
Belt	*Ibéti*
Shirt	*Ishéti*
Powder	*Ipóda*

Foods/cooking

Tomatoes	*Itomátosi*
Stove	*Isitóvu*
Gas-cooker	*Igásíkuka*
Kerosine	*Ikrasí*
Maggi cube	*Imagí*
Kitchen	*Ikíshini*
Biscuit	*Ibisikíti*
Milk	*Iminíki*
Butter	*Ibóta*
Bread	*Ibrédi*
Mango	*Imaigolo*
Pawpaw	*Ipopó*
Pineapple	*Ipanaipolo*

Medical staff/establishment

Doctor	*Idokíto*
Nurse	*Inósi*

Hospital	*Esipíto/Osipito*
Mortuary	*Imóshúarhi*
Legal terms	
Lawyer	*Inoyá*
Magistrate	*Imágístreti*
Judge	*Ijóji*
Court	*Ikótu*
Prison	*Iprisíne*
Personal names	
Jesus	*Ijísosi /Ijésu*
John	*Ijôni*
Moses	*Imósisi*
Alice	*Anísi*
Comfort	*Ikofótu*
Margaret	*Imagréti*

It is thus seen that borrowing of words from English to designate objects, which are new or relatively new to the people has been a very productive process. This also can be seen in the expression of ideas. Here English verbs are also borrowed. Many Urhobo do not know the local equivalents of such verbs as:

'set' in 'set or switch on the radio'
'fry' in 'fry the meat'
'stew' in 'stew it all'.

In situations necessitating the use of these words many Urhobo would not shy away from them and others of their type. Every language has her own purists, and there are in Urhobo. It is to be noted that the sixteenth century English opposed most of the loaned words which they termed 'inkhorn terms'. A similar situation is noticeable among Urhobo purists. National consciousness and linguistic integrity have prompted (what in linguistics is called *calquing*) the formation of local equivalents to the already borrowed, reformed and accepted English words. Thus for

Car	they form		*Okórotó*
Aeroplane	``	``	*Okerénu*
Television	``	``	*Ékpetirúghe*
Radio	``	``	*Agboró*
Teacher	``	``	*Oyonihwo*
Church	``	``	*Uwevwirega*
Judge	``	``	*Obrórhie*

Like English itself, the Urhobo language has had loans from neighbouring language. Thus

Eba (Yoruba) for *Igarí*

Olopa - Yoruba for *Ipolísi*
Ube - Yoruba for *Ólúmu* (pear)
Aganuzo – Ukwani for *Owidjerhe*

The combined impact of the contact with English and the dynamics of cultural evolution have of necessity led to innovation in ideas, practices and artefacts - a fact which has rendered long held ideas and beliefs questionable, if not ridiculous, and expedited the relegation of long cherished household objects into desuetude. This strand of socio-cultural development has led to the loss of many words in the language and is still, in fact, threatening quite a number of others. A number of such words and what they designate are given below:

Uvweruvwe	-	uncircumcised penis
Emerúe	-	a special mat for disposing house refuse
Ovákpo	-	widow
Oyoromo	-	nursemaid
Idoró	-	cupboard
Ekété	-	bamboo-bed
Okidiumúkpe	-	oil lamp
Ukoro	-	coral bead worn on the foot and hand by women
Uwuye	-	perforated iron sheet for grating cassava
Umuanmwa	-	girdle for keeping money used by women
Ogeróbo/orárá	-	ladle
Isegede	-	a mud house yet to be walled with mashed sand

The socio-economic progress of the people and tastes, imbibed from contacts with other people, have led to the abandoning of such words. Today many houses now have a specially enlarged brass spoon to show for a ladle (*ogerobo*). Many women, in place of a girdle, now have specially sewn U-shaped bags strapped to their waist with a zip on top for keeping their money. Modern women talk of bags. This wind of change affected many areas of life. In the sphere of health and health care such words as '*ifi*' (a kind of pronounced body rashes) has died along with the disease itself. In the monetary field a lot of change has been recorded. Interest has shifted from the cowrie a unit of monetary value to pounds and shillings and today people talk of naira and kobo. Some of the words rendered out of use in these changes are:

anini	equivalent	to	¼ kobo
apini/epini	``	``	½ kobo
obovo	``	``	1½ kobo
utoro	``	``	3 kobo
ichibe	``	``	6 kobo
inayi	``	``	9 kobo

In the area of games and recreations, there are morphological structures left stranded and lying waste in the journey through history. Among these are *ahwe, uto-* (games by boys) and *apa* games more enjoyed by girls. In the area of marriage, modern trends in monogamy are confining such words as *Avwebo* (often confused as *Amebo* with the influence of a neighbouring language) *Avwiorovwe* and *Ayada* to the stock of archaisms.

In her turn English has experienced this phenomenon where words are rendered obsolete in course of cultural evolution. Today the English word 'sweg' has been totally supplanted by 'noise', 'wered' by 'crowd' and we are a witness to how 'wed' (now confined to invitation cards) is giving way for the word 'marry', a French loan.

Apart from the English loans which are recognized and cited above, there are others, which cannot be said to be loaned yet used in Urhobo either unconsciously or as a betrayal of poor performance in the language. Especially among the educated Urhobo people, one hears such English words as 'so', 'because', 'but', 'and' etc in their spoken Urhobo. These can hardly express themselves without resorting to this 'code mixing'. To this extent one can justifiably say that such words as cited above have been found handy in the Urhobo language.

Like the rest of the indigenous languages in the country, it is hardly arguable that Urhobo cannot be used as a medium of instruction in our educational system and this is just one among many areas of language usage. This is because there are very many concepts in English which are yet to have equivalents in Urhobo. Hoe does one interpret concepts such as latitude, longitude, equator, osmosis, photosynthesis, metathesis, apocope among many in Urhobo. It can be seen that a lot of work, either unconsciously or consciously is called for if Urhobo is to be able to verbalize the concepts and innovations of the present day. What is true of Urhobo is to varying degrees true of the other Nigerian languages. This is one among many reasons why the question of a national language will be intractable for a long time.

It must however be quickly pointed out that "judgements of backwardness (Ferguson) or limited development of a language cannot be made on the basis of linguistic structure (but on the basis of development." By development he means the extent of *graphization*, i.e. reduction to writing; *standardization*, i.e. the development of a variety which overrides regional and social dialect, and *modernization*, i.e. the development of inter-translatability with other languages in range of topics and forms of discourse characteristic of industrialized, secularized and structurally differentiated modern societies.

Shedding light on a similar topic Unoh (1990) discusses the various developmental stages a language must undergo before it is considered modernized. These as explained by him are:
i. They are characterized by well-developed, modern and standard orthographies;

ii. They are characterized by well-developed and well-attested traditions of written literature of various kinds;
iii. They are characterized by systematically developed meta-language, technical terms and other specialized vocabularies for effective communication or information dissemination in various fields of human activity and learning;
iv. They have dictionaries, encyclopaedia and other reference sources that are suitable for use at various educational levels;
v. They are not only taught but also used for instructional communication at all levels of formal, non-formal and informal education;
vi. They have several well-developed instructional materials, including comprehensive descriptions of the grammar, which could aid their teaching and learning at all educational levels; and
vii. There are several well-trained experts (including linguists, literary scholars, language artists, language educationists, lexicographers and others) to promote and guide various aspects of the enrichment and use of the language.

It is clear from these canons that the Urhobo language is yet to be on course for rigorous linguistic and scholarly development.

Perhaps Williamson makes the best point on the development of any language when she admonished the minority language groups that '... the fate of small languages is in the hands of their speakers. If they wish their language to grow and develop, they should take steps not only to *use* it themselves but to ensure that their children are adequately exposed to it and retain it as their home language to pass on to the next generation.'

Works cited

Barber, C.L, *The Story of Language*, PAN Book Ltd, London S.W.I. 1965

Ferguson, C.A., *Language Structure and Language Use*, Stanford Univ. Press, Stanford, California, 1971.

Ofua, Akpomedaye, *Eta Urhobo: Urhobo News and Cultural Magazine*, No. 2 Vol. 2, 1990.

Otite, Onigu, *The Urhobo People*, Heinemann Educational Books (Nig) Ltd., 1982

Robins, R.H., *General Linguistics: An Introductory Survey*, Longman Group Ltd; 1980.

Sadjere G. U., *ETA: An Urhobo Cultural Magazine,* 1980

Unoh, Solomon O., 'The Development and Use of Nigerian Languages for a Taxonomy of Communicative functions,' a paper presented at LANS 11th annual conference at the University of Calabar, 1990.

Williamson, Kay, 'Reading, Writing and Publishing in Small Languages,' in Rose Aziza and Nolue Emenanjo (eds.), *Teaching Nigerian Languages: Experiences from the Delta,* Emba Printing and Publishing Company Ltd., Onitsha, 1992.

7

Urhobo kingdoms and dialects

— *W. Onoriose*

Introduction

Urhobo is an ethnic group comprising twenty-two polities or clans. The polities/clans, arranged in alphabetical order, are Agbarha, Agbarha-Ame, Agbarho, Agbon, Arhavwarien, Avwraka, Eghwu, Ephron-Oto, Evwreni, Idjerhe, Ogor, Okere, Okparabe, Okpe, Olomu, Orogun, Udu, Ughelle, Ughievwen and Uvwie. Each of these clans constitutes an autonomous society, which claims descent from a common ancestral origin. Almost all Urhobo clans have kingship systems with the exception of a few where governance is through gerontocracy. The autonomous nature of the clans makes each of them a kingdom.

The Urhobo name borne by these disparate kingdoms might be misconstrued to mean that all Urhobo people are a monolithic group of individuals who descended from one eponymous ancestor. There are no chronicles to help in the reconstruction of the history of the Urhobo people to ascertain whether the word 'Urhobo' was the name of a particular individual or an expression for the identity of the people as an ethnic group. There is also the absence of archaeological findings to assist in authenticating the identity of Urhobo. The only source of information available to anyone interested in Urhobo studies is the oral traditions of the various kingdoms. Oral traditions, as we know them, are fraught with uncertainties, inaccuracies, falsehoods and deliberate embellishments, which exert limitations on the extents to which they can be regarded as truths. However, in our quest for the genesis of the Urhobo people, we are left with no alternatives than to resist the limitations inherent in oral traditions and depend on them if we must develop the outline of the origin of the Urhobo people.

The Urhobo kingdoms

Onigu Otite, N.Y. Nabofa, S.U. Erivwo and G.G. Darah have undertaken what amounts to a collation of the traditions of origin of the various Urhobo kingdoms. I am indebted to these writers for the information I have used in this chapter.

Certain distinct facts emerge from the various traditions of origin of the Urhobo kingdoms. One of these is the enormous and incessant reference to the Benin kingdom. Oghwoghwa, the ancestor of Ogor, Ughelle, Agbarha and Orogun kingdoms, is said to have come from Benin. The traditions showed that he took an eastern route, which brought him to the River Niger, which he followed downwards. His marital contact with the Ijo in the Delta area preceded his final settlement some distance from the swamps of the Delta. His immediate progeny founded Ughelli, Ogor, Agbarha and Orogun kingdoms. There was dispersion in the Agbarha kingdom, which resulted in the emergence of Idjerhe, Oghara and Agbarha-Ame. A diasporic phenomenon similar to that of Agbarha also erupted in Ughelli kingdom. Ughelli-Urhie communities, which are the visible expressions of that occurrence did not constitute kingdoms of their own. They identify themselves as part of Ughelli kingdom although spurious political boundary delimitation some years ago grafted them to Ijo area of Patani Local Government Area where they are treated as minority elements.

Apart from Oghwoghwa, the other Urhobo kingdoms also claim migration from Benin. Abraka in particular, is said to have left Benin for its present location. Abraka kingdom is the only Urhobo kingdom that does not narrate any tradition of not having settled midway at any time before settling in her present location.

Unlike Oghwoghwa whose children became the founders of the kingdoms named after them, the other immigrants from Benin personally founded the kingdoms named after them. Kingdoms that developed in this manner include Eghwu, Ughievwen, Okpe, Evwreni, Ughwerun, Udu, Okparabe and Arhavwarien.

Another clear fact from the traditions of origin of the Urhobo kingdoms is the relationship between most of the founding fathers and the Ijo people in the course of their migration. Oghwoghwa, as has been mentioned earlier, married an Ijo lady during his brief stop over in the Tarakri area of the Ijo country. Marriage is also said to have taken place between Olomu people and the Ijo of Kiagbodo. Eghwu, Udu, Arhavwarien and Okparabe kingdoms are said to have emerged after some relationship with the Ijo before they finally settled in their present locations. According to G.G. Darah, who narrates the account of the origin of the Udu kingdom, the word 'Udu', which the kingdom bears, was the name of an Ijo woman. It is significant to note that many of the Urhobo migrants resided briefly at Ogobiri, an Ijo territory, in the process of their search for suitable and secure places for settlement.

The other point that can be elicited from the stories of the founding of the kingdoms is that a few of them trace their origin to Igbo and Isoko. N.Y. Nabofa who narrates the story of the founding of Evwreni kingdom states that some Evwreni people claim to have originated from Igbo country. Okpe, Agbon and Ughwerun kingdoms assert close kinship ties with Isoko.

From the various accounts, it is possible to infer that the twenty-two kingdoms of Urhobo did not emerge from a single individual. If one immigrant had been the founding father of Urhobo, he would have evolved a homogenous community with one royal father as in the case of the Benin Empire. The different manners and time of arrival, and the different waves by which immigrants moved into the area are factors that must be taken into cognisance in the discussion of Urhobo dialects. The role of ethnic groups, which are contiguous with the various Urhobo kingdoms should also be recognised as contributing to the diversity of dialects found in Urhobo language.

Urhobo language

All Urhobo people speak and understand one universal language called Urhobo language. For a people who have emigrated from diverse directions at different times, to speak and understand a common language needs some explanation. There have been no philological studies of the Urhobo language to explain the origin and expansion of the language. Certain questions become pertinent in the search for the genesis and growth of the Urhobo language:

i) Were there aborigines on the land whose language was Urhobo before the advent of the foreigners from Benin, Igbo, Ijo and Isoko?
ii) If most of the founding fathers of the twenty-two kingdoms migrated from Benin, as their traditions suggest, why was the Bini Language not dominant after the amalgamation of the new entrants into the area?
iii) What is the cause of the diversity of dialects in the Urhobo language?

Whatever explanation one may attempt for these questions can only be speculative. There is no authentic answer to the first question. That there were aboriginal Urhobo living in the area before the incursion of the new comers into the area has not been authoritatively declared. However, the oral traditions of the Olomu people and those of Eghwu maintain that there were some Urhobo aborigines in these particular areas before foreigners came there. Some of the aborigines at Olomu, according to Nabofa, were over-powered by Igboze who "used his Benin influence to suppress the Urhobo aborigines that he met." At Eghwu there were some aboriginal people also who lost their identity to the strangers. Common sense would make us to know that definitely the immigrants were quite many. Therefore, the possibility of their dominating their hosts cannot be doubted. But how the Urhobo language survived in spite of the overpowering presence of the new people can be explained that it was the only means of communication between the natives and the foreigners. The new comers probably learnt the language of the aborigines before they began to suppress them.

The answers to the second question on why the Benin language could not gain prominence over and above the language of the hosting communities can partially be explained in terms of distance and permanent separation of the immigrants from their original homes. This linguistic reality recognises distance as one of the causes of differences of a language at the centre and the same language at the periphery. The farther away a language is from the core area the less intact the language becomes. A typical example is the American English that became very different from English language due to the distance that separated the two regions. Perhaps, the circumstances that caused the migrants to depart from their original homes were so harrowing that they had no qualms losing their original language. Such a people could be non-nostalgic in their feeling towards such a language and would develop a tendency to acquire a new language.

In the course of time, such a people may become completely oblivious of their original language. They may, however, preserve some words, phrases or expressions, which would continue to exist in the new language. This could be the reason why some words in the Bini language are found in Urhobo language. "*Igho*", "*ọmọ*", '*ese*' meaning 'money', 'child', 'blessing' and many others, for example, are pronounced the same in Urhobo and have the same meanings also.

One other point still demands mentioning in the explanation of the possible wearing off of the Bini language. Most of the Urhobo kingdoms' ancestors who were claimed to have migrated from Benin bore names that sound alien to Urhobo listeners. "Oghwoghwa", for example, has no association with any Urhobo experience in life. From Urhobo perspective "Oghwoghwa" could mean either "a load carrier" or "a money sprayer". Africans, unlike other races such as Europeans, Asians, Chinese and Indians, give names that are experientially meaningful.

The Urhobo meanings of the word could not have been what Oghwoghwa's parents meant when they gave him the name. The words 'Avwraka', 'Agbon', 'Eghwu', 'Ughwerun', and Ughievwen sound more of Bini than Urhobo names. Digraphs and consonant clusters like "gb", and "gh" noticed in the formation of the names are frequently seen in the Bini language. On the other hand, names like Afiesere, Ufuoma, Uduophori, Adjekota, Oteri, etc., clearly indicate Urhobo expressions with reasonable meanings. One can say that in giving names to people, places and objects, the new settlers shifted from Bini to Urhobo language as the latter was gaining ascendancy over their Benin language that was already suffering atrophy.

All the Urhobo kingdoms speak a general Urhobo language. This is very important as an instrument of cohesion among the kingdoms. The people refer to the area as Urhobo nation. The Urhobo nation is both a political and a social unit for them and their loyalty to their nation is greatly sustained by the single linguistic code by means of which their communication is carried out.

Urhobo dialects

Our third question we asked somewhere above will be answered in the discussion that follows. There are twenty-two dialects in the Urhobo language in consonance with the twenty-two kingdoms or polities in the area. A dialect an Urhobo man speaks indicates the kingdom he hails from. Food, dressing pattern, marriage system, administrative system and religious observances are nearly the same throughout Urhobo land. Farming and palm collecting are the traditional occupations of Urhobo people. People in kingdoms located in riverine areas undertake to fishing as an additional occupation. Burial ceremonies are organised the same way through out the twenty-two kingdoms. In all aspects of culture all Urhobo people behave alike. Outside the dialects, it is extremely impossible to distinguish an Agbarha man or an Udu man or an Ephron-Otor man from a man from Ughelli, Abraka, Olomu or any of the other kingdoms.

In their definition of dialect, Andrew Schiller, Doris Welch, Ralph Nicholas and William Jenkins (1972:356) say that "A dialect is a variety of a language that differs from other varieties." They added further that "A dialect is a specific variety of language spoken by a group of people in a particular geographic location."

The definition stated above explains the relationship between the Urhobo language and the various dialects. Urhobo is spoken, understood and written by all Urhobo people. However, it should not sound ambiguous to assert that there is no core Urhobo language. This observation had earlier been noted by J. Kelly (1969:153) when he remarked that "Urhobo is spoken, in various forms, over most of Urhobo division." A dialect spoken in any one kingdom can be understood by people from other kingdoms. Thus someone from Orogun kingdom can understand another person who speaks Eghwu dialect but he cannot express himself in Eghwu dialect. When, therefore, we say all Urhobo speak Urhobo language, what we actually mean is that all Urhobo people understand one another irrespective of the kingdom they hail from. No Urhobo man from one kingdom can speak the dialect of another kingdom except he had been trained to speak the other dialect. This is corroborated by Schiller (1972: 356) *et al.* when they say "people who speak different dialects of the same language can understand each other" Femi Akindele and Wale Adegbite (1999:22) hold a similar view when they opine that "The dialects of a language are mutually intelligible to all speakers of the language."

According to Schiller *et al.*, there are two kinds of dialects. One is regional dialect and the other is social dialect. A regional dialect is determined by the geographic location of the group of people who speak the dialect. A regional dialect gives a clue as to where someone has lived. Somebody who speaks Agbon dialect would be easily identified as an Agbon person.

A social dialect differs from a regional dialect. The former is determined by such factors as social status and education. The English language has three levels of social dialect. These are (1) Standard English (2) Popular English and (3) Non-Standard or Folk dialect. In Urhobo, a social dialect is non-existent. This is because the social structure of Urhobo people is not stratified along any line. Wealth and education do not cast any differentiation in the speech system of the people. The only difference noticed in the language of Urhobo people is the one between the elderly people and the younger ones. In the speech of older people there is profuse use of proverbs and wise sayings, which may be absent from that of the younger people. All the dialects of Urhobo language have equal status as varieties of the language. As George Yule (1996:228) puts it "no variety of a language is better than another."

The cause of the existence of dialects of the language, which is our third question, can be explained in terms of what George Yule (1996:217) regards as "language change". According to him, a language changes diachronically and synchronically. A diachronic change is due to the historical changes that occur in the life and language of a people over time. A synchronic change, on its side, relates to "The differences within one language in different places and among different groups at the same time". The diachronic theory would explain the evolution of the dialects to have been occasioned by the history of the immigrants into the area. Their movements to their final settlements in Urhobo land took several years. They mingled with several people before their permanent settlement with the aborigines. Since the movement was not a mass exodus of people but by some small families, each settlement they made developed its own aspect of the Urhobo language.

The synchronic theory can also be employed to establish the growth of the dialects. They had probably emerged in a manner one can presume to be concurrent. Each of the kingdoms had settled in an area in which some inhabitants were already present. The Orogun people had settled close to the Ukwani and by this their variant of the Urhobo became affected. Oghara and Idjerhe kingdoms were residing contiguously with the Benin and Itsekiri. These people equally brought some modifications in the Urhobo spoken by them. Agbon and Okpe kingdoms claim descent from Isoko. Although they do not leave close to their ancestral people, they claim to have many things in common and sometimes exchange of visits is made between them. Ughelli, Ogor, Eghwu, Arhavwarien, Okparabe, Ughweru, Udu and Ughievwen claim kinship with the Ijo who are their next-door neighbours. No doubt the Urhobo language spoken in these kingdoms cannot escape some alteration in terms of pronunciation, lexical items and syntax. For example the fish, which Agbon and Abraka call '*obra*' is called '*otomi*' in those kingdoms close to Ijo country. The same is true of the fish called "*onigu*" in in-land Urhobo kingdoms but which is called '*ogono*' by the Ughelli-Urhie people. The Ijo people call it '*ogono*'.

The existence of dialects in a language rests on such linguistic features as pronunciation and accent, lexical items, and syntax. An examination of each of these features will reveal the role it plays in the existence of dialects in the Urhobo language.

The pronunciation of some words by people from some kingdoms exhibits the variety noticed in the language. Ughelli, Agbarha, Ogor, Eghwu and Arhavwarien people pronounce the English word 'mortar' "*udo*". However, people from Agbon, Okpe, Agbarho, Udu and some others call it "*urho*". '*Udo*' and '*urho*' are phonetically transcribed as /udo/ and /uryo/ respectively. Similarly the former group of kingdoms call 'town', '*odo*' while the latter group of kingdoms says '*orho*'. What obtains here is the use of either the /d/ or /ry/ allophone by different kingdoms. Abraka, Agbon and Okpe people call 'bag' '*ekpu*' while Eghwu, Arhavwarien and Okparabe people call it '*akpa*'. While people in Abraka kingdom would make the sentence "*Keme ekpu me*" meaning, "Give me my bag", people from most other Urhobo kingdoms would say "*Kevwe ekpu/ akpa me*".

At the lexical level the differences are equally glaring. The English word 'soup' is called "*oghwo*" in Agbon and Abraka, while most other kingdoms call it "*irhibo*". Ughelli; Eghwu, and Arhavwarien kingdoms call 'umbrella' '*asasa*'. In Abraka and Agbon kingdoms it is called "*ekharha*" while in Ughievwen and Udu kingdoms it is called "*achicha*". The personal pronoun 'me' in English means "*meme*" for Arhavwarien and Abraka people, while people from other kingdoms say '*mevwe*'. The word 'cutlass' is known in different ways in Urhobo. In some kingdoms it is called '*oda*'; in some others it is '*opia*'; and in the rest it is '*agada*'.

The ways words are accented also indicate dialectal differences. In expressing the English concept 'no', Ogor, Abraka and Orogun people would say "`ejò`", while Eghwu and Arhavwarien would say "*ájò*". In the first case the initial and final syllables have falling accent, while in the second case the initial syllable has a rising accent and the final syllable has a falling accent. The phrase "my own" has a similar manner of expression. Ughelli, Idjerhe and Oghara people would say '*ò mê*' while Eghwu and Arhavwarien would say "*ò vwè*". In this instance, the former has the first and second syllables having falling and rising accents respectively. In the latter example the two syllables have falling accents.

At the syntactic level, much of the dialectal differences are also encountered. One example among the innumerable expressions of the kind is used here.

Udu/Ughięvwen	Translation
1(a) *O whosa vwę* Agbon/Ughelli	He/She paid me a debt Translation
1(b) *O whę osa kę vwę*	He/She paid a debt to me

In sentence 1(a) the structure is Subject + Verb + Indirect Object + Direct Object. In sentence 1(b) the structure is Subject + Verb + Direct Object + Indirect Object. We can see that although expressions 1(a) and 1(b) carry the same meaning, they are grammatically different. An Ughelli speaker will not make the sentence made by the Ughievwen speaker although both of them understand thoroughly what is expressed.

Another syntactic feature unique to the Udu and Ughievwen speakers is the practice of the elision of prepositional items as in the case of '*ke*' in the example of sentence 1(a) above. They also practise the elision of initial vowels in the names of persons. Names like 'Nyorere', "Siakpere", and 'Rukevwe' have been subjected to the elision of their initial vowels. The actual names are Enyorere, Isiakpere, Erukevwe, respectively.

An interesting thing about the various dialects is their mutual intelligibility to all Urhobo speakers. The exceptions in this regard are the dialects spoken in Okpe and Ephrǫn/Uvwie kingdoms. People in these two kingdoms can speak and understand Urhobo clearly but people from the other twenty kingdoms cannot understand or speak both Okpe and Ephrǫn dialects. They, thus, can be regarded as different languages. In this respect, they meet the postulations of Akindele and Adegbite (1999:22) who say, "a dialect which is not intelligible to other people constitutes a language of its own."

Of all the dialects of the Urhobo language Agbarho dialect has a unique nature. Agbarho kingdom is zone of convergence of many Urhobo people. According to Otite (95), Agbarho is said to be "the amalgamation of several Urhobo people." Agbarho community is therefore a mixture of different Urhobo people who migrated from Eghwu, Ughievwen, Ughelli and Uvwie. Agbarho dialect is made up of contributions from others dialects, a phenomenon which makes it standard and central for people from different parts of Urhobo to understand easily.

Conclusion

The origin of the various Urhobo kingdoms, the language and the dialects cannot be explained in isolation from one another. A study of the language moves abreast with the study of the dialects. Dialects on their part create the territorial demarcations of the kingdoms. For now the accounts of the origin of the kingdoms are only being derived from oral traditions. Efforts should be made to embark on archaeological endeavours to help in the process of authentication of the oral traditions. Through such efforts much would be unearthed about the kingdoms, language and dialects of Urhobo people.

Works cited

Akindele, Femi and Wale Adegbite, *The Sociology and Politics of English in Nigeria: An Introduction*, Ile-Ife, Obafemi Awolowo University Press Limited, 1999.
Darah, G.G., "Udu" in *The Urhobo People*, Onigu Otite (ed.), Ibadan, Heinemann, Undated, pp. 173 –182.
Darah, G. G., "Ughiẹvwen" in *The Urhobo People*, Onigu Otite (ed.), Ibadan, Heinemann, Undated, pp. 183-194.
Erivwo, S.U., "The Oghwoghwa Group of Urhobo, Ogo, Ughelli, Agbarha Oto and Orogun," in *The Urhobo People*, Onigu Otite (ed.), Ibadan, Heinemann, Undated, pp. 29-50.
Erivwo, S.U., "Oghwoghwa Diaspora: The Ughelle-Urhie People," in *The Urhobo People*, Onigu Otite (ed.), Ibadan, Heinemann, Undated, pp 51 –55.
Erivwo,S. U., "Idjerhe", in *The Urhobo People*, Onigu Otite (ed.), Ibadan, Heinemann, Undated, pp. 56-62.
Haughen, E. "Dialect, Language, Nation," in J.B. Pride and Janet Holmes, eds., *Sociolinguistics*, Harmondsworth, Penguin Books, 1979, pp 97-111.
Kelly, J. "Urhobo" in *Twelve Nigerian Languages*, Elizabeth Dunstan, ed., Ibadan, 1969, pp. 153-160.
Malmkjaer, Kirssted, ed., *The Linguistics Encyclopaedia*, London Routledge, 1995.
Nabofa, N.Y. "Ughwerun" in *The Urhobo People*, Onigu Otite, ed., Ibadan, Heinemann, Undated, pp. 84-97.
Nabofa, NY, "Eghwu" in *The Urhobo People*, Onigu Otite, ed., Ibadan, Heinemann, Undated, pp 183-194.
Nabofa,NY, "Okparabe" in *The Urhobo People*, Onigu Otite, ed., Ibadan, Heinemann, Undated, pp. 146-155.
Nabofa, N Y, "Arhavwarien" in *The Urhobo People*, Onigu Otite, ed., Ibadan, Heinemann, Undated, pp. 156-165.
Otite, Onigu, "On sources and the Writing of History without Records," in *The Urhobo People*, Onigu Otite, ed., Ibadan, Heinemann, Undated, pp. 4-7.
Otite, Oghara, "Oghara" , 'Agbon', 'Uvwie' 'Okpe 'Avwraka', in *The Urhobo People*, Onigu Otite, ed., Ibadan, Heinemann, Undated.
Schiller Andrew, Doris Welch, Ralph Nicholas and Williarn Jenkins, *Language and Communication*, Glenview, Illinois, Foresman and Company, 1972.
Yule, George, *The Study of Language*, London Cambridge, 1976.

8

Urhobo culture and the challenges of modernisation

– G.G. Darah

Introduction

In the past few decades, the ideology of capitalist individualism has overwhelmed much of the democratic institutions of social control and mobilization. Some of the things that helped to define Urhobo national identity have either been discarded or are under severe threat from forces of change and modernization. We can now examine some of these changes as they affect the Urhobo and their capacity to reproduce and propagate their civilization.

The view of "culture" which restricts it to elements of arts and religious practice is inadequate for our purpose. The most comprehensive definition of the term is that offered in the 1988 *Cultural Policy for Nigeria.* Sections 1.1 to.1.3 of the *Policy* define culture as:

1.1 The totality of the way of life evolved by a people in their attempts to meet the challenges of living in their environment, which gives order and meaning to their social, political, economic, aesthetic and religious norms and modes of organization, thus distinguishing a people from their neighbours.

1.2 Culture comprises material, institutional, philosophical and creative aspects. The material aspect has to do with artefacts in their broadest form (namely, tools, clothing, food, medicine, utensils, housing, etc.); the institutional deals with the political, social, legal and economic structures erected to help achieve material and spiritual objectives; while the philosophical is concerned with ideas, beliefs and values; the creative concerns a people's literature (oral or written) as well as their visual and performing arts which are normally moulded by, as well as help to mould other aspects of culture.

1.3 Culture is not merely a return to the customs of the past. It embodies the attitude of a people to the future of their traditional values faced with the demands of modern technology which is an essential factor in development and progress.

These four fundamental aspects of culture are present in Urhobo experience. Urhobo material culture is manifested in the form of technological tools and objects *(ekwakwa akpo-eyeren)* such as cultlass *(agada/opia)*, axe *(ushurhen)*, *oko-edi* (oil palm refinery/factory), climbing rig *(efi)*, *oko* (canoe, vehicle, vessel), chair/seat *(agbara, ekpeti), uwevwin* (house)

The holistic definition shows that the term *culture* includes economy *(uweren/emuenduo)* science *(iroro ona)* technology *(ekwakwa ona/ona eghie)*, construction *(echihon/ebon)* architecture *(uwevwin echihon)*, estate development/town planning *(orere efan)* politics *(isuesun)*, philosophy *(iroro okokodo)* ideology/belief *(iroro akpo/ega)*, marketing/trading/commerce *(eki-echuo)* advertising *(emu eghoro/emu-eshe/eghwoghwo)*, values/custom *(uruemu)*, history *(ikun awaren)*, education *(iyono/ebe eyono)* writing *(ebe esio)* counselling *(uchebro/iroro ema)* judgement *(edjo/egwon/edjo/orhien ebro)* arts *(eha/onyevwen)*, literary art/stories/narratives *(esia/ikun egbe)*, songs *(ine)* dance/performance *(igbe/eha)*, drumming *(ihwahworo)*, oratory/speech *(ota-eta/iyeren,* broadcasting *(ota eghwoghwo/eyorhe)*, proverbs/idioms *(ise)*, fine arts *(isiasi ona/ekakare/omama)*, weaving *(erhuon)* fashion *(osevwe)*, culinary arts *(emuechere/uchere)*, reception *(egho, edede)* athletics *(one edje)*, wrestling *(abo emuo)*

We can now highlight a few areas of cultural stress and challenge for the Urhobo.

Urbanisation

The growth of urban centres has redefined the economy, demography and cultural outlook of the Urhobo. The process started in the last decade of the nineteenth century with the founding of Sapele and Warri around 1891. These towns were established by the British for the purpose of achieving effective administration and to promote trade and commerce. Their location at the strategic points along the two major rivers of Warri and the Ethiope was an advantage to the British and other sea-faring nations of Europe. By the 1920s, the two cities had been classified as Grade B townships along with places like Benin, Ijebu-Ode, Ibadan, Abeokuta, Jos, Zaria, Makurdi, Calabar, and Owerri. Other smaller townships and administrative centres that were developed in Urhobo include Ughelli, Abraka, Okpare, and Orerokpe. The population of Warri and Sapele was very mixed before the 1960s but became predominantly Urhobo during the 1967-70 Nigerian Civil War when Igbo immigrants fled to their rebel enclave.

Good planning and sanitation were ensured before and during the colonial era. The influx of Urhobo and other Nigerian immigrants since the 1970s has overcrowded the cities and turned them to ghettoes and slums. This poses a cultural challenge. The Urhobo used to be noted for their high taste in environmental sanitation and traditional architecture. Their villages are well laid out, cleaned regularly and provided with spaces for religious and artistic expression. Orchards of trees and food crops are an integral part of our rural settlements. The Urhobo immigrants in *ukane* have been able to replicate this aesthetics in their work camps. In fact, Chief Thompson Edogbeji Atkins Salubi, a foremost Urhobo nationalist and President-General of the Urhobo Progressive Union (UPU) from 1961-1983, began his civil service career as a sanitary inspector in Lagos. He later specialized as an industrial relations technocratic and represented Nigeria in the council of the International Labour Organisation.

It would seem that the Urhobo have lost control of their urban spaces. Warri and Effurun are particularly notorious for congestion, flooding, and disease-infested tenements. Part of the reason for this chaos is that the capitalist ideology of profit motive or what the Urhobo call *igho she emu sua* has overwhelmed our time-honoured reputation for neatness, order, and elegance. The drive to make money from land has led to uncontrolled sale of spaces, including strategic cultural spaces. For example, the only sacred cultural sanctuary probably surviving in Effurun now is the *Edjuvwie* temple by the waterfront. In Warri, only the Agbarha shrine/temple has escaped demolition by property developers.

The fastest-growing Urhobo emerging town now is Abraka. Here, the jungle culture in Warri and Effurun and environs is being replicated. Chunks of land are appropriated; flood plains are converted into residential apartments without any drainage system and when the rains invade, tenements are made inaccessible and treacherous to dwellers. Neither the Ethiope East local council nor the Ministries of Lands, Surveys and Urban Development nor of Environment is involved in the process at Abraka.

There is, therefore, an urgent need to produce a master plan of Urhobo urban centres. Urhobo cultural symbols, theatres for performances, congregation, decision-making, leisure, and games should be integral parts of this urban renewal programme. At least one major Urhobo cultural festival or fiesta should take place in all the cities yearly in order to replenish cultural energy and stamp Urhobo cultural consciousness on the population. Urban housing should display icons and symbols of Urhobo identity and artistic imagination.

In all Asian cities, which are as modern as New York, London, and Paris, murals of religion, arts, and philosophy are proudly advertised. The dragon, which is a religious totem in parts of Asia, is represented in public and private buildings, manufactured items, and computer games. The Koreans who produce one-third of electronic equipment in the world honour their ancestors by providing space for their veneration in museums, parks, homes and places of worship and work. With their advanced technology and globalized outlook, the Koreans still consult spirit mediums and ancestral forces before undertaking a marriage or risky business. Most times, communication with these metaphysical agencies is conducted via the computer and Internet.

The Urhobo will not lose self-esteem and religious piety if they adopt some of these modernizing techniques. I propose that place names and traffic signs in major cities should be written in Urhobo language and ideographs. Airports, motor parks and waterfronts should be provided with artistic billboards, souvenirs, travel guides/maps, and general purpose books on elements of Urhobo civilization. The Urhobo will earn greater respect from the world community this way than by the export of oil and gas.

It is gratifying that Governor Ibori's administration has produced an urban renewal master plan for what will turn out to be DELTA OIL CITY. It will comprise thirty-two settlements, including Warri and Effurun. No less than ninety per cent of the territory will be in Urhobo. The Urhobo should produce a design of how their culture, traditional architecture, language, arts, aesthetic taste, games/leisure, and festivals can dominate the new city. All that is required is to study the master plan and submit proposals on how to integrate these landmarks of Urhobo civilization into it. I have identified some of these projects in my 2001 paper, "Warri and Its Global Sisters".

Language and the loss of identity

Illiteracy and deafness in Urhobo language are some of the negative consequences of urbanization. The situation since the 1970s has been so bad that there are now several generations of Urhobo children who neither understand nor speak Urhobo. This is tantamount to act of cultural suicide. The danger is made more graphic by the fact that Igbo and Yoruba immigrants in Urhobo cities are able to speak their native tongues. The alternative of Delta Pidgin is a communicative necessity, but it is not a substitute. Most Urhobo children raised in urban environments can now only utter the common greeting: *minguo* (*miguọ*) ("I am kneeling down") If you answer with "*Vren do, mavọ?*" ("Rise up, how are you?") you will get a blank and a bewildered look. This *minguo* (*miguọ*) generation does not have the capacity to understand and transmit the essentials of culture and civilization that can give the Urhobo identity and esteem in the global community of 6,000 languages.

This is an emergency crisis that demands the resources of a cultural war. Communicative competence in the language of one's culture is the only lasting credential that entitles one to membership and citizenship of that cultural universe. All human beings share similar attributes of biology/anatomy, reproduction, loving, dressing, being rich or poor, and getting ill and dying. Language is the single most important element that distinguishes one people from another. The imperative of multi-lingualism has a divine sanction in the Biblical story of the building of the Tower of Babel. Language is the most dynamic curator and transmitter of culture. It is the software of civilization. Indeed, to speak is both divine and human.

It had been observed that Urhobo is among the ten largest of Nigeria's 398 languages. How can this premier status be sustained when the language is dying as a medium of communication and instruction? Modernisation is not an excuse for this cultural disaster that has befallen the Urhobo nation. The Chinese language of HAN is spoken by about one billion people, that is, one-sixth of the human population. The Chinese economy has been the fastest-growing in the past ten years. Yet the Chinese still speak and write their languages whilst undergoing modernization. The Japanese, Koreans and Indians are advanced in technology. They learn it in their native tongues and use them to name and market their industrial products throughout the world market.

Once again, it is the Urhobo in *ukane* Diaspora who have taken worthy initiatives to tackle the language problem. The Lagos-based Urhobo Foundation has set up a language school in Yaba area of Lagos. The Atamu Club, another Lagos-based group, sponsored the publication of the first comprehensive Urhobo dictionary in 2001. The lexicographer is the Okpe-born Ayemenokpe Edward Osubele, a teacher at the Federal Government College, Odogbolu in Ogun State. The Urhobo Social Club, also in Lagos, runs a weekly Urhobo discussion programme on a channel of the Nigerian Television Authority in Lagos. The take-off in 2002 of the *Wadooh* magazine in Urhobo by the publishers of *Urhobo Voice* is a revolutionary step. These noteworthy efforts demonstrate how seriously the Urhobo Diaspora takes the language challenge.

The self-help spirit that opened frontiers for the Urhobo in education in the 1940s should now be reinvented to advance a cultural crusade. Clubs should spearhead the development of a viable Urhobo degree programme at the Delta State University, Abraka. A well-equipped language laboratory, instructional materials, and competent teachers are needed urgently for the programme to earn the accreditation of the National Universities Commission. Fortunately, the Department of Languages and Linguistics is headed by Dr. Rose Aziza, the first Urhobo to do a doctorate degree in Urhobo language at Ibadan in 1997. Whilst at the College of Education, Warri, Dr Aziza promoted Urhobo language studies. In 1993, 47 students registered for Urhobo in the National Certificate of Education. Among the students were those from Edo State. Students offering Isoko and Izon (Ijo) enjoyed scholarships. Chief J. Erhirhi gave scholarship awards to all thirteen Isoko students at the time. The Bomadi local government did the same for all twenty-five students studying Ijo. There was no similar effort by the Urhobo at the time.

For several years now, the Urhobo degree programme at DELSU has not got the patronage of students. Most parents and their children do not think that it is worthwhile to go to university to study Urhobo. Yet thousands of Urhobo children scramble yearly to enter congested courses such as law, banking and finance, medicine, engineering, and management. Some are happy to read

French or German which are of no immediate advantage to them or Urhobo. Of the thirty or so students registered for introductory Urhobo courses at DELSU, no more than half is Urhobo by birth. Nearly all of them are "deaf" in Urhobo. Most of them cannot write the language because they were not taught in schools, including those situated in Urhobo territory.

The various Urhobo clubs should make their independent intervention in the matter and mobilise resources to promote serious academic studies of Urhobo culture and language. All Urhobo local government councils must be compelled by a UPU directive to make budgetary allocation for the promotion of Urhobo language and culture. Reading materials, children's computer games, video/film and souvenirs in Urhobo should be available at affordable and subsidized rates.

The local councils and Urhobo philanthropists should sponsor programmes on radio and television. The use of Urhobo language in these media should extend beyond translation of news first written in English. Serious intellectual debates and controversies should be conducted in Urhobo language on all aspects of life, including politics, economics, law, philosophy, science, technology, diplomacy, arts, literature, energy, environment, youth.

Abridged histories of major events and achievements of the Urhobo people and their heroes/heroines should be available in Urhobo and translations in order to inspire the younger generation to venerate them and strive to surpass their accomplishments. Cartoon books, illustrated folktales, adventure stories, science fiction, and computer games should be produced in Urhobo language and symbols to attract the interest of urban-based children. The local councils and clubs should sponsor writing and debating competitions in Urhobo and also encourage inventors and designers to use the medium of Urhobo to promote and explain their inventions/designs to potential manufacturers.

Conclusion

The Urhobo ended the nineteenth century with the chains of British colonialism clamped on their feet. But the Urhobo refused to be subdued. The Urhobo lived through most of the twentieth century with the double yoke of Itsekiri, Yoruba, and Hausa-Fulani sub-imperialisms on their necks. The Urhobo did not choke but instead struggled valiantly and asserted their national identity and sovereignty.

Urhobo achievements in the fields of education, enterprise and politics in the last few decades are worthy compensation for the toils and trials of the past. As the Urhobo enter the new capitalist "global village" of the twenty-first century, they are certain to become one of the groups that will change the destiny of the world in radical and revolutionary ways. That optimism is robustly expressed in the Urhobo national anthem:

Kokoko o gbare
Urhobo e, orere ivie esan
Ko ko ko o gbare
Urhobo e, orere ivie esan
Eke Urhobo je vwe na
Orere ofa je vwe otioyen ha-o
Edefa me cha akpo
Oto Urhobo me hwan rhe
Urhobo e e e e
Orere ivie esan
A rie oma-ooo.

Arise, arise, it is time
Urhobo, land of multitudes
Arise, arise, it is time
Urhobo, land of freedom
My love for Urhobo
Surpasses that for any other land.
Whenever I reincarnate
will do so in Urhobo land
Hail Urhobo
Land of multiples and freedom
In unity we stand.

9

Urhobo proverbs and axioms

– Tanure Ojaide

A proverb is a wise saying that expresses an idea in a concise and succinct manner. It is a traditional trope or saying that is highly figurative. It tends to have a central image that is expanded upon to convey meaning. For instance, in the saying *"Erako v'akaba gbi ghwre evu r'aghwa-a"* (A dog with bells will not be lost in the bush), the central image is of a dog wearing bells whose ringing will always expose its whereabouts. Similarly, *"Ichi eni bẹ evughe-e"* (The elephant's footprints are not difficult to recognise) has the size of the elephant as its central image. The proverb generally exhibits wit and is usually anonymous in the sense that it cannot be attributed to a single individual or persons. Its origin is always ancient, even though, as will be shown later, some proverbs appear to be much older than others because of the conditions of the time in which they were introduced into the language. Proverbs are language and ethnic-based and often result from generations of observation or experience. Every proverb appears to emanate from experience over a very long period and seems at a particular time to be incontrovertible truth or perceived truth from observable reality.

However, while proverbs are deeply rooted in traditional culture in which they play many roles such as advising, cautioning, and entertaining, they arise from the people's experience and sensibility. They reflect the character of a people or an ethnic group since they affirm acceptance of what the proverbs entail. The way of life or lifestyle that is not acceptable to a people cannot be corroborated by their proverbs. The ethics, morality, and virtues of a people are enshrined in their proverbs. To the non-literate Urhobo, for many ages, their proverbs became the memory of their common experience as a people. After all, language is the most important carrier of a people's culture. With the Urhobo people, the strength of their language lies in the proverbs, which are not only expressive and communicative tools but also agents of the perpetuation of their entire culture and its values.

A people's culture and experience are dynamic and change with time. With the Urhobo language, as time changes, so do new proverbs come up to express and reflect the new realities. Proverbs, to the Urhobo people, are the summarization of keen observation and lessons learnt from different facets of life. In Urhobo, as in many African languages with similar experience, there are traditional and pre-colonial proverbs, which arose from traditional living conditions. Such proverbs, as will be exemplified later, tend to adopt the traditional mode of knowing and seeing things. A small ethnic world, the observations that make the proverb tend to be narrow in scope and some could with new sensibilities be questioned as in gender issues of the patriarchal Urhobo people.

There are other proverbs, which can be termed post-colonial and modern, which resulted from the new life that came with the contact with Europeans and their values. The Urhobo, for centuries, have had contact with Europeans, especially the Portuguese and the English. As in the essay on the evolution of the language shows, the Urhobo language is highly indebted to the Portuguese and English languages. Resulting from the contact with Europeans are proverbs or axiomatic sayings such as "That I wear short knickers does not mean that I have short sense." There is also the proverb associated with the police, a post-modern institution in Urhoboland - as one rises in the police profession, the smaller and smarter one's gun becomes. Proverbs, therefore, continue to be formed by people about their experiences. The proverb is an integral part of the language, which carries it to enrich and strengthen itself.

What is amazing in Urhobo and other languages world-wide is that a proverb is never assigned to a person and it is rare to know specifically from where in the language belt that it derives. An Urhobo proverb could be more used in one area than another, but still it is never said to be, for instance, an Udu or Agbon proverb.

As just stated, it is extremely rare to locate a proverb within an area in which the language is spoken. However, such specificity could relate to legends or practice over a period. Put simply, certain legendary happenings and social observations become proverbial in some areas. In Okpara, it is said "*T'arhe t'akpo, Saduwa ore Aka*" (After all is said and done, Saduwa is an alien). Saduwa, according to legend, was a highly influential man in Okpara who exercised much power. He could not be king because he was seen as a foreigner. Also, there is the saying all over Urhobo that "*Ifada rien obo ro rue Okurekpo*" (The reverend father knows why he stays put at Okurekpo.) This arose from the time Catholic priests were just coming to Urhoboland. Though Okurekpo was a village and the pastoral home was a hut, yet the fathers preferred living there because they were well taken care of there than they would be in bigger towns like Okpara Inland, Okpara Waterside, or Eku. The priests also resisted being transferred from Okurekpo. It is now proverbial to see somebody sticking to an apparently less appealing place for some secret reasons.

Since a people's experience involves their environment, history, culture, society, politics, character, sensibility, and world-view, proverbs relate to these diverse and broad manifestations of human experience. Proverbs are used to register the people's ethos and affirm faith in their own ways of life.

The Urhobo have experienced much in their migration from the eponymous "Aka" (Benin) to where they are today. Their settling down in the mangrove and rain forest areas of the Niger Delta, the occupations that the environment conditioned them to take to, and their subsequent lifestyles also go on to make their ethnic experience. As it is said, "*Edje ogo k'orhua-a*" (You don't show the grass-cutter where cultivable land is). It is its natural haunt. One is always familiar with one's own environment. Also, "*Asa r'adia, oye avwe ebe r'oye vware oko.*" (It is leaves that you find where you live that you use to wrap what you have). These two proverbs, among many others, show the significance of the environment in a people's lives. Correspondingly, since the people's lives are being expressed in proverbs, their proverbs are rooted in the environment.

The Urhobo environment involves the climate, vegetation, and the fauna and flora of the place. Urhobo proverbs are couched and grounded in the physical environment. The images or figures that are central to any proverb are parts of the living realities of the people, things they see or perceive in their homeland. For instance, "*Obuko iyeke, iyeke da zoro*" (It is at its back that the *iyeke* shows its gracefulness). It is also said that "*Ugboduma ose r'eya na*" (The *ugboduma* scenting leaves are favourites of women). This shows how women like good things or things that make them more desired. Both *iyeke* and *ugboduma* are examples of the use to which people make of their environment in forming their proverbs. Proverbs, like images, derive from the people's environment because it is what one knows that one uses to express oneself.

What are the occasions for the likely use of proverbs in Urhobo? The Urhobo people like good speakers and communicators. As will be discussed of the *otota*/traditional orator, effective verbal communication is a sign of good leadership. One can mobilise, engage or disengage with facility of proverbial expression. A good speaker is expected to possess oratorical skills and, thus, copiously and effortlessly employ proverbs. Among the Urhobo, one who speaks effectively with proverbs is usually chosen or appointed as *otota*, spokesperson, of the family, group, village, quarter, or town. There can be an ad hoc spokesperson (*otota r'ikpregede*), who presents and receives drinks and kola nuts on behalf of a group. It is a position of honour as a good speaker or orator is usually chosen to lead a delegation to represent a side in contention with another. The person is expected to communicate with oratorical skill that can make him or her smoothly navigate difficult and thorny issues and present in an acceptable manner the views of his or her side. Knowledge and spontaneous use of proverbs are the sine qua non in the performance of the duty of the *otota*, any leader, or adult in Urhoboland.

So, any occasion that involves speaking the language calls for the use of proverbs in articulating one's views to press home the relevant points. In particular, any gathering in which projecting views, arguments, or persuasive skills are involved tends to elicit the use of proverbs. The strength of one's ideas can only be conveyed through the use of powerful language. In traditional Urhobo society, powerful language always involves the use of proverbs.

Occasions of land disputes, family, or town meetings, burial arrangement discussion, bride-wealth and other traditional marriage rites, and other socio-cultural occasions call for the use of proverbs. Adults talking, parents talking to children, husband and wife talking at home, and other occasions demand reinforcement or fortification of points, which proverbs bring about. There are, for instance, factual statements such as "*Oke yara je ọgọrọ ga*" (As time elapses, palm wine gets stronger) to express negative change as time goes on. In this case, the younger the sweeter. In other words, youthfulness has benefits that disappear with age. This could apply to men and women who may be less likely to bear children compared to when younger. Also, to the Urhobo, the woman is more appealing when young than when older. Another proverb derived from factual observation is "When an old person loses a tooth, it doesn't grow back." Also, "*Osevwe r'omotete f'ọkpako-o*" (A young person's dress does not fit an old person). It appears, therefore, that Urhobo proverbs can either be figurative language or extended images or familiar observed phenomena.

While old people tend to use proverbs more, a facility gained from life experience, sometimes relatively young adults also have good command of proverbial language. After all, it is not the length of life that matters, but its achievement! And, "*Orọyare mrẹ ne orọtọre*" (The person who travels wide experiences more than the sedentary old). Those who are more likely to make use of proverbs are professional *ọtota* (spokespersons), the old, and the naturally gifted. As explained earlier, there are occasions, which demand the use of proverbs and they could be out of place when an adult is talking to a small child. The mood of the place is also important. When there is bereavement, for instance, certain philosophical proverbs could be used to console the grief-stricken. On the other hand, certain festive occasions calling for conviviality will also need the use of proverbs.

One can divide Urhobo proverbs into the following groups or patterns: daily or regular conversational proverbs; medicinal/ritual/religious proverbs; social and special occasion proverbs; and philosophical proverbs. The proverbs used daily and informally form a vast repertory of oratorical, rhetorical, and figurative language. One hears a mother lamenting her child's stubbornness with "*Okpọmọ eni vwiẹ*" (The elephant delivers a big offspring). I have heard somebody who has many children tell critics that no matter how big the teeth, the mouth still carries them!

I will focus on the later three categories of proverbs. Many rituals and religious activities call for invocations and incantations, which are usually proverbial in nature. Many medicine men and healers use proverbs in their prayers and consultations. There is, for instance, *"Obo obaro ogoro pho ra"* (The frog only jumps forward) used to promote the idea of progress, as opposed to retrogression. Also, to impress on a person an accident-free journey, the healer says *"Egbede wa ne, oruru ki tighe"* (The needle passes the fabric before the thread gets entangled). In addition, *"Ekpere owhe, j'owhe wa"* (You can't stop the seasons). In this direction, *"Edo whe urhe-e"* (Noise does not kill a tree). A land of many birds, Urhobo forest trees would have all gone if noise could kill them. These and more proverbs are special ways that healers imbibe certain powers or virtues onto their patients. And, because proverbs are concise and ancient, they tend to be favourite aspects of ritual discourse. The proverbs used in rituals are generally very pointed in the expression of an idea. This is very apt since prayers and rituals are directed and seek specific needs to be fulfilled and proverbs provide the language to achieve them.

There are also proverbs that tend to be used on a daily basis and also on social occasions. To the traditional Urhobo person, a poor person's child does not go to attend a festival in England. In the catfish's gathering, it is difficult to tell the young from the old because everybody wears a beard. To express the uniqueness of every occasion, *"Orẹ vwerhe re, j'asa wo worin"* (A festival's enjoyment depends on your hosts). While the Urhobo tend to be republican in outlook, there is a general deference to age and wealth in the society. Many proverbs reflect and express the social attitudes and character of the people. Socially, who has a boy and a girl has had all the children one needs to have: in this case, male and female children. The rich-poor class division in Urhobo society can also be discerned from many proverbs.

Many proverbs derive from the philosophical sophistication of the Urhobo. Also derived from experience, such proverbs express the experience, observation, and knowledge of the people. Like many proverbs, they tend to be factual statements whose truth cannot be contested in traditional reasoning. To many, *"omonoge che te ovware"* (The young sapling shall grow into a tall palm tree). Also, *"Ukpe te k'eruemu ukpe"* (Each year brings its own demands). To the Urhobo, "Two hands a man always has" (*Abọ ive evwo*). This means there are two sides to every person: the father's and the mother's sides respectively.

There are proverbs in Urhobo used to advise and caution people. One is expected to seek advice rather than think and act alone. Hence, *"Owho ọvo da j'iroro, k'ọye nẹrhe odue oni r'ọye."* The elders ask for patience from young ones in *"Oki rhie esuẹ aye rh'ọrhare, ane okri nọ."* If one has been a bachelor all one's life till the age of marriage, why should a day's delay before his wife joins him be a problem?

Other proverbs ask for tolerance, unity, and good behaviour to others. In the need to rally people together in a time of crisis, *"Okposio da rho egbo, t'eredekọ t'eravwe r'awha ki rue unu ọvo"* (When there is a big storm in the bush, snakes and other animals seek shelter in one available hole). It is in appreciation of what the axe has done that it is borne shoulder high ("*Obọ ushurhe ru k'owho, oye evwo mwo igabọ*"). Also somebody cannot be carrying an elephant and be digging for a cricket. Too many things distract, unlike just one; hence "*Ubi ọvo ghwre erhare-e.*" Prices of products do not always depend on the whims and caprices of the trader/seller. That is why "*Obe oku ughwerin ghare nurhe*" (Salt prices are determined from the sea source). A child that will not allow its mother to sleep will also not sleep. To many elders, instead of having a weakling for a child, it is better to have a successful thief ("*Ukpe evwo vwie ozue, evwie oji*"). And how long does one live to spend a long time in a hut? In other words, one should enjoy oneself when the means are there.

Proverbs form part of the "deep talk" of Urhobo. While some expressions are deep, they are not necessarily proverbs. For instance, when an intruder comes into a private meeting, one says "*Isọ otọ*," which really means that there is excrement on the ground and one should tread carefully not to divulge secrets. A saying such as "*Eya ri kpori j'ughere*" (The woman who is leaving marriage is still at the outskirts of town). This statement shows that the woman is reluctant to leave. These are wise says but may not be in the corpus of proverbs.

Proverbs are very important in Urhobo oratory. While there are many more skilled in the use of proverbs, every adult and good speaker of the language is expected to master its use to be seen as fully proficient in the language. The proverb foregrounds a statement by making it very clear to understand figuratively. It is an expression that is common but so witty, knowledgeable, and succinct. It gives colour to expressions, which, by being poetic, is intellectually stimulating. It, thus, conveys in an entertaining but figurative way the wisdom of the Urhobo people over the ages.

While modernity has informed some proverbs, modern experience could question some traditional assumptions expressed in proverbs. Let me give two examples. The Urhobo say, as quoted earlier, that "*Wo rhua iruo ọnọkpa, je ọhwunu rẹ krẹ vwiyọ*" (As you advance in the police profession, the smaller and smarter the gun you carry). From the people's experience, the bigger officers have short guns (shotguns) and rifles, unlike the recruits and corporals with big Dane-like guns. This is definitely a post-modern proverb. Also the Urhobo, a patriarchal people, say "*Ohoro ọvo hwe oshọ*" (One woman kills a man's sexual appetite.) This proverb justifies Urhobo polygamy. A more balanced gender-sensitive society will question the proverb. It is too much of one thing, without variety, that causes boredom or lack of appetite. However, couched in male chauvinistic terms, this proverb again reflects the Urhobo character.

No doubt, proverbs give colour and intellectual spice to the Urhobo language. The so many proverbs attest not only to the richness of the language but also to the various experiences of the people. Above all, from the proverbs, you will know the Urhobo people.

10

Linguistic correlates of 'salvation' in Urhobo religious cosmogony

– D. V. Jike & S. O. Ogege

Introduction

Unique linguistic characterisation and religious beliefs are major factors that distinguish one culture from another. Though language might be distinctive to each particular ethnic group or a linguistic belt comprising several ethnic groups, the linguistic nomenclature and belief systems of a people are generally known as cultural universals i.e. they are found across cultures. Religion as an aspect of the supranational consists of a system of beliefs, thought and probable action that are traceable to the prevailing cultural ethos. It is a set pattern of responses to the unknown, comprising a kaleidoscope of happenstance and uncertainties that are not easily amenable to rational thought. Stark (1987:352) has defined religion as "socially organised beliefs and activities offering solicitations on questions of ultimate meaning."

Religion is synonymous with a sacred canopy or a sheltering fabric hanging over a people, giving them security and providing answers to the fundamental questions of life (Berger, 1967). Religion answers pertinent questions like why people suffer or eschatological questions like where people finally end up when they die. Religion possesses a capacity that non-religious philosophies lack: to invoke the power, wisdom, authority and aid of the gods (Spiro, 1966; Berger, 1967; Stark, 1981, Stark and William, 1985). In a nutshell, religion is the prevailing cosmic reality. However, religion cannot provide a comprehensive framework for most of this interpretation and must as a matter of necessity rely on the linguistic element of a culture. Generally, language refers to a set of symbols that express ideas and enable people to think and communicate with one another. It may be verbal (spoken) or non-verbal (written or gestured).

Whichever form a language may take; it expresses not only our thoughts but conveys a critical synergy between our collective perception and our leverage of influence over social reality.

If the linguistic characterisations of a people actually shape their collective worldview, then some aspects of our world and immediate milieu must deserve more illuminating attention. One such pertinent aspect is the linguistic characterisation of salvation among the Urhobo of southern Nigeria. More aptly, this essay is pre-occupied with the linguistic correlates of salvation in Urhobo religious cosmogony.

The Urhobo people in history

The Urhobo ethnic nationality is made up of about twenty-two territorial and socially contiguous groupings, comprising eight local government areas in Delta State, Nigeria. The actual origin of the Urhobo is tied to multiple traditions. Otite (1982) maintains that there are about four traditions of origin. These traditions are not mutually exclusive because they tend to reinforce one another. However, since the traditions of origin of the Urhobo people are not germane to the thrust of this paper, we shall ignore them. Nonetheless, we shall briefly examine the population strength of the Urhobo people. The population census of 1991 stipulated a figure of 1,090,409 for the Urhobo people. According to the census records, the Urhobo nation occupies a land area of about 2,000 square miles and lies roughly within latitudes $6°$ and $5°$ North of the equator and longitudes $5°$ 40 and $6°$ 25 East of Greenwich Meridian (Onokerhoraye, 1980). The Urhobo shares a coastal region with the Ijaw, Itsekiri and Isoko while Ukwani and Benin are to the North of Urhobo territory.

The linguistic history reveals that the Urhobo people speak the Urhobo language, a language that belongs to the Kwa group of languages. Rather than dwell on the etymology of the language, we shall quickly highlight the linguistic correlates of salvation in Urhobo religious cosmogony.

The concept of salvation

Generally, the concept of salvation is often perceived in contradistinction with its biblical correlate – to be saved. The whole of the Old Testament is a brisk narrative of a suffering people whose ultimate salvation hinged on absolute obedience to and faith in a messiah who was yet to come but whose coming was prophesied rather profusely to make every one yearn for him. In a nutshell, the New Testament is, more or less, a fulfilment of the prophecies of the Old Testament especially those relating to the emergence of the messiah in the physical form of Jesus Christ. The ministry of John the Baptist heralded the coming of the Messiah. John enjoined all who cared to listen to repent for the kingdom of God was at hand (Luke, 3:3 – 4). Jesus Christ the Messiah was the physical manifestation of that kingdom and repentance for the remission of sin was the cardinal qualification one required to be part of the kingdom.

The eventual emergence of Jesus Christ is accompanied with a blitz of scriptural reiteration and re-affirmation of this predominant condition for attaining salvation, a word which is more or less a synonym of the kingdom of God. Jesus Christ states rather emphatically that "I am the way, the truth and the life, no one cometh to the father but by me" (John 14:6). In another breath, Jesus re-asserts that you cannot attain salvation unless you are born again. According to this biblical doctrine, you must be born of water i.e. baptism by immersion, a significant symbolism of the death and resurrection of Christ and the other condition is that you must be born of the Holy Spirit, i.e. a spiritual renunciation of the sinful characteristics of the old nature of man. The new convert must forge ahead in spiritual tandem with the unblemished Christ by thoroughly repudiating everything that is worldly, evil, sinful or dissonant with the prevailing Christian ethos. Old things must pass away.

By contrast, linguistic correlates of salvation among the Urhobo resonate with the mundane rather than the metaphysical. There are no rigid beliefs on a transcendent spiritual existence after death in a Godly kingdom that is far removed from the general perception of the day to day existence of the people. They will say – *'Ufuoma akpoeyere'* literally translated means peace is the basis of existence or peace is synonymous with salvation. This is perhaps coterminous with the basic philosophy of African life as illustrated in the works of several African writers including, (Hountondji, 1983, Gyekye, 1988; 1996; Masolo, 1995 and Nyasani 1999). In a nutshell the Urhobo linguistic correlate of salvation is largely predicated on a characteristically African philosophy of existence, which showcases peace as a central plank. Peace precedes salvation and is the basis for its continuing reification. Among the Urhobo, salvation is not something to be yearned for and prepared for at a much more abstract spiritual plane. Salvation is right here and now and is rather metaphorically ambidextrous having spiritual and physical dimensions which are so pervasive and germane to the religious cosmogony in several rituals associated with rite de passage (Mbiti, 1969; Appiah, 1987; Osei, 1971).

The man is saved who is doing well and leading a societally agreed upon good life, consisting of a sanctified patrimony and an unfettered ability to meet social obligations to one's nuclear family and to exterior members of one's extended family network. He is saved who has several wives in a well entrenched tradition of polygyny with many offspring's in tow even when the man is not able to see them through school. Salvation is immediate, urgent and almost fatalistic, for example *ekpe ede ano* and *to-ode* meaning salvation is a daily affair and may you make tomorrow respectively. To attain salvation there is a tendency for the Urhobo to offer sacrifices to a range of unseen forces.

Sometimes sacrifices of chickens or goats *(izobo)* are made at crossroads for individual peace to reign or for an impending harm to be deflected away from a set target. People also make sacrifices as a form of deliverance from the tormenting spirit of witches *(erieda)* or mermaid spirit *(olokun)*. At certain times, large trees are venerated, offering sacrifices of dry fish *(utseri)* and palm oil *(ofigbo)* around such tree trunks especially if there were a revelation that such a tree was a significant rendezvous for spiritual powers in high places. The resort to sacrifices is a form of spiritual cleansing and rejuvenation to ensure individual and collective longevity (salvation here on earth). Charms or amulet may be worn when embarking on a journey. Sometimes fetish objects are hung on the lintel of a house with a firm conviction in the intrinsic ability of the fetish object to ward off opposing evil forces.

The Urhobo perceive life and death as two sides of a long continuum in human existence. They place a preponderant premium on life, living it to the fullest and, by so doing, indulging in several vices that pose formidable obstacles to the attainment of biblical salvation. But these very obstacles, drinks *(ogogoro)*, polygny and general fun are the evident criteria of the good life and salvation among the Urhobo. There appears to be a historic dualism between this world and the other world. The human person is generally believed to belong to this world. If there are fluctuations in his earthly fortunes, efforts are quickly made to consult oracles or forbears who are believed to have attained the status of pantheons to ensure that they remain in this world. Even when there is a biological evidence of death, it is often described linguistically as a journey. *Okpoya* meaning that the deceased has embarked on a short journey. The dead among the Urhobo are well dressed before they are lowered down. Sometimes valuables like jewellery and even cooking utensils are left in the casket in order to facilitate the so-called journey by the decreased into the unknown. There is a general belief among the Urhobo that the physical body of the dead decomposes while the soul proceeds on an interminable short journey'. Through the process of *eri-nere* (spiritual transformation) beatification rites and subsequent remembrance ceremonies, the dead is nostalgically labelled *ugbeyako*. This is more or less, analogous to Mbiti's (1969) 'living dead'. Life in the perception of the Urhobo is cyclical in nature. The linguistic correlate of this belief *akpo-vwo ba-a* – literally translated means life is interminable. The emphasis on an earth-bound salvation is even reflected in the concept of re-incarnation, which is basically a transposition of the souls of the dead into living beings in the world of existence. This is classical reincarnation in Urhobo cosmogony. It is also a parallel, although unbiblical variant of being born again. The soul of a dead person transposes into the miniature form of a newly born baby with features remarkably similar to a dead sibling within the genealogy. The re-incarnated are generally believed to have come back to complete unfinished business in a world that is replete with eternally transcendent features of salvation. The linguistic reflection of the concept of re-incarnation among the Urhobo is *aromarhe* meaning they have come back to life. Parallel concepts among the Yoruba are *Babatunde* (father has returned) or *Yetunde* (mother has returned). The pervasive belief in reincarnation by the Urhobo is even embodied in a popular dirge during funeral rites:

Eh – ote – ote
Eh – ote – ote
Wo vwo ya ne
Oko re igho vwo
Ko ye wo rua
Oko re emo vwa
Ko ye wo rua
Ote – ote

What this simply means is that when returning to life in the two-way journey of salvation, the dead should endeavour to board the ship of wealth and children. Wealth among the Urhobo is encompassing including money, property, wives and children. There are other recognisable status symbols like chieftaincy titles. However, the point must be highlighted that there are divergent perspectives on these issues among the Urhobo. Some people are of the view that the '*otacha*' (destiny) of a person remains the same even in death. These people argue that wealth, poverty, intelligence and physical, configurations like the colour of skin or the sex of a person in the other world remain the same as it is in this world. They maintain that although the soul is separated from the body in death, life in the other world is, more or less, a replica of what it was in this world. In a nutshell, there is a general belief that the physical and social characteristics of the individual's life in this world are retained by the transposed soul in the other world.

The converse viewpoint is that as soon as deceased persons cross the Rubicon of physical existence, they shed all worldly physical characteristics and acquire other characteristics that bear little or no resemblance to the earthly ones they once possessed. Thus a deceased young girl could re-incarnate with features and physical characteristics of a long- departed forbear. The dirge occupies a significant place in Urhobo religious cosmogony. First, to provide encouragement to the living of the inevitable fate that awaits them; and, secondly, to facilitate the journey of the deceased into the unknown. It is, more or less, a complex reciprocal and paradoxical gesture where the living wishes the dead prosperity and the living pours libation to the dead and makes relevant supplication for the dead to bless them (the living) in return.

Linguistic symbolism

The Urhobo also express salvation through myriad forms of symbolism. Linguistic symbolism is a way of communicating cosmic experience through non-verbal linguistic expression. Symbol, according to Jung (1979), refers to an image or picture that we are familiar with in our daily life yet possesses specific connotation in addition to its conventional and obvious meaning. Nabofa (1994) aptly captures the meaning of symbol as an overt expression of what is behind the veil of direct perception.

The Urhobo people communicate their inner cosmic experience through *erhi* or *oma* – symbols for the souls of ancestors that depict salvation. These symbols are usually of varying shapes depending on the intrinsic and inherent salvational message it is meant to convey. It could be *epharo-ivẹ* (Janus head) two human faces in opposite direction. This portrays a symbolic existence or representation in both worlds of a deceased person. A father may be physically dead but exists in the spiritual realm where he oversees the living and the dead in a much more perceptive and panoramic way than when he was alive. The symbol of the father figure looks into the past and the future and is able to co-ordinate the fortunes of family members when called upon to do so through rituals of enervation and atonement.

The point must be reiterated that while worldly salvation is generally sought by dint of hard work and the acquisition of material possessions are illustrative examples of salvation, the dead achieves sustainable salvation by a constant replenishment of a welter of rituals. Sometimes an ancestor within the pantheon may refuse to be active especially if offsprings have failed to meet traditional obligations of annual remembrances/ceremonies. In this particular situation, the dead still enjoys the status of immortality but it has transposed further into a spiritual realm where it no longer has communion or interaction with the living. The spiritual transformation is linguistically referred to as *okpen oro-re ugbenvwere* meaning the dead has relocated to an innermost part of the other world where it no longer guides and protects its progeny from opposing evil forces.

Conclusion

The concept of salvation in Urhobo religious cosmogony is different from the biblical teachings on the subject. According to the Christian doctrine, the human environment is a preparatory ground for those who choose a righteous lifestyle to separate themselves from the vast majority of those who crave after materialism. The righteous, who seek after kingdomly objectives in tandem with the biblical doctrine, would pass through the eye of the needle and be saved. The others who are preoccupied with worldly cares would be damned and like the biblical injunction, it would be easier for the camel to pass though the eyes of the needle than for these people to be saved. Rigid conditions must be met before Christians would be saved. Not so in Urhobo religious cosmogony where the concept of salvation is linguistically diffuse, part here and part hereafter.

People equate salvation with the good life characterised by wealth, wives and titles even when they are acquired in perfidious circumstances. Premium is placed on salvation here on earth and any threat (health-wise) to this earthly status is vigorously addressed by an avalanche of rituals, divinations and ancestral supplications to restore one back to full health. In death, the departed often proclaimed among the living and is remembered in several ways including the pouring of libation especially to solicit the continual spiritual vigilance of the dead over the living. The dead is on a temporary journey to the unknown and is often expected back in the people's mythology. There is a cyclical tapestry of a firm criss-cross between the living and the dead. Much of what is known as salvation in Urhobo religious cosmogony is celebratory. There are no dire consequences for sinful behaviour and there are no rigid prescriptions for the most desirable way to salvation (Silvoso, 1994; Sjogren, 1997; Haggard, 1995).

References

Appiah, K (1987) "Old Gods, New Worlds: Some Recent Work in the Philosophy of African Traditional Religion," in G. Floistad, ed., *Contemporary Philosophy: A New Survey*, Vol. 5, African Philosophy, Dordrecht: Martinus Nijhoff.
Berger, P.L. (1967) *The Sacred Canopy*. Garden City, N.Y. Doubleday.
Gyekye, K (1988), *The Unexamined Life: Philosophy and the African Experience*, Accra: Ghana Universities Pres.
Gyekye, K (1996), *African Culture Values: An Introduction*, Philadelphia and Accra: Sankofa Publishing Company.
Haggard, T (1995) *Primary Purpose: Making it Hard for People to go the Hell from your City*, Orlando, FL.: Creation House Press.
Hountondji, P. (1983) *African Philosophy: Myth and Reality*. London: Hutchinson. Bloomington: Indiana University Press.
Jung, G. C. (1979), *Man and His Symbols*, London, Jupital Books.
Mbiti, J. S. (1969), *African Religions and Philosophy,* New York, Praeger Publishers.
Mosolo, D.A. (1995), *African Philosophy in Search of Identity,* Nairobi: East African Publishers.
Nabofa, M.Y. (1994), *Symbolism in African Traditional Religion*, Ibadan PaperBack Publishers Ltd.
Nyasani, J.M. (1997), *The African Psyche*, Nairobi: University Press.
Onokerhoraye, A.C. (1980), *Bendel: A Survey Resources for Development*, Ibadan: NISER.
Osei, G.K. (1971), *The African Philosophy of Life*, London, The African Publication Society.
Otite, O. (1982). *The Urhobo People*, London, Heinemann Educational Books.
Silvoso, E.. (1994). *The None should Perish: How to Reach Entire Cities for Christ through Prayer Evangelism*, California, Reyal Books.
Sjogren, S. (1997) *Servant Evangelism: Kindness Campaigner in Loving Your Way into the Kingdom*, City Reaching Strategies for a 21st Century Revival, 131–134 Venture: Regal Books.

Spiro, M. E. (1966), "*Religion: Problems of Definition and Explanation,*" in Michael Banton, ed., *Anthropological Approaches to the study of Religions,* New York Praeger, pp. 85-126.

Stark, R. (1981) "*Must All Religions be Supernatural?*" in Bryan Wilson, ed., *The Social Impact of New Religious Movements,* New York: Rose of Sharon Press, pp. 159-177.

Stark, R, and William S. B. (1985) *The Future of Religion: Secularisation revival and Cult Formation,* Berkeley, University of California Press.

11

Urhobo gospel music

– *M. Mowarin*

The objective of this chapter is to examine the role of Urhobo gospel music in the propagation of Christianity among the Urhobo. Religion is a feature of man's existence. Among the Urhobo, the transition from traditional African religion to Christianity has not diminished the complementary role of music in the propagation of religion. Music is central to many aspects of Urhobo life since it is an integral part of their life. Music stimulates the Urhobo imagination and shields them from the drudgery and vicissitudes of everyday existence. Among Urhobo Christians, music is now a central feature of worship.

Urhobo is one of Nigeria's minor languages and it is among the one hundred languages spoken in the South South geo-political zone of Nigeria (Egbokhare, 2001:115). The Urhobo constitute one of the major ethnic nationalities in the Niger Delta and they are found predominantly in Delta State and partly in Bayelsa State. Otite (1980) is of the view that the Urhobo constitute the fifth largest ethnic group in Nigeria after Hausa, Yoruba, Igbo and Izon (Ijaw). Aweto (2002:1) gives an estimate of the population of the Urhobo thus: "The population of Urhoboland was 1.2m in 1991. Today, the population is about 1.5m." Aweto (Ibid: 1) gives an apt description of the location of Urhoboland thus:

> Urhobo land is located in the Western part of the Niger Delta, South of latitude 6"N it is a contiguous territory of about 5000 square kilometres in the Southern part of Delta State of Nigeria. It is bounded by latitude 5^0 15" N and longitudes 5^0 40"S and 6^0 25"E.

Elugbe (1978:4) states that Urhobo is a member of the Edoid family of languages which is a member of the Kwa branch of the Niger Congo family of languages. A majority of the Edoid family of languages is spoken in Edo and Delta States and they fall into four primary sub-groups. They include Delta Edoid (DE) South Western Edoid (SWE), North Central Edoid (NCE) and North Western Edoid (NWE). Elugbe (Ibid: 8) further adds that Urhobo falls under the SWE sub-group which is further sub-divided into five regional groupings. They are the Eruwa, the Isoko (Igabo), the Urhobo (Sobo), the Okpe and the Uvbie (Evhron Effurun). Out of the five groups, Elugbe observes that the Isoko and Urhobo are the largest.

Otite (*op. cit.*, 9) identifies seventeen dialectal variations of the Urhobo language and the dialects are identified through the major towns in which each of the dialects predominate. Elugbe (*op. cit.*, 21) observes that the SWE area has two lingua francas. While the Agbarho dialect is the lingua franca in the Urhobo areas of Okpe and Uvwie, Uzere dialect is the lingua franca in the Isoko and Eruwa areas.

Aziza (1997) quoting Elugbe (1977, 1978), states that Urhobo is a terraced level tone system with two basic tones *high* and *low* two gliding tones *high-low* (falling) and low-high (rising). These two gliding tones are derived from the level tones.

Urhobo gospel music is used as a vehicle for spreading the gospel. Most Urhobo people are non-literate rural dwellers who can neither read nor write in English or Urhobo. The dogma of Christianity is embedded in some of the songs. Likibe in "*Omini mini*" exalts the name of the Christian God above other gods thus:

Oghene yo'mini mini	-	God is Omnipotent, Omnipresent and Omniscience
a mre enu rhe vwo je vwe	-	There is nothing to compare you with
we yi ma akpo ve ojuvwu nana	-	You created this earth and heaver
Oghene y'ovie rive	-	God is king of kings.
Makashe rho'juvwu o	-	Angels in heaven
Aye jiro orho vwo'hwo na	-	They praise our Lord.
Jesu Kristi o no'juvwu re re o	-	Jesus came from heaven
Mre asa ri je uvie rho'ghene vwo	-	So that he can be opportuned to show
Ki iwo rha akpo	-	Human beings the glory of heaven.
Jesu vwo re ko re tane	-	When Jesus came he told
Eki sio bo ni umemu rere ojuvwu	-	Us to give up sin
Na mra sa te avware obo	-	So that we can inherit eternal glory.

God, Jesus Christ and the angels, who are the heavenly beings that Urhobo Christians worship are glorified and exalted in the song above. Jesus' plea for repentance by Christians as a prerequisite for enjoying the transcendental dimensions of existence and inheriting the kingdom of heaven are also illuminated in the song above. This song briefly annotates the theme of Christian religion.

Another function of Urhobo gospel music is its use as an instrument to influence the behaviour of Urhobo Christians. The need to live a pious life and renounce sin is a recurring decimal in this regard. Moulding human behaviour is one of the common features of Christian religion as well as other religions.

The Urhobo gospel singer Ofurie in *Uvie Rodjuvwu oye orere ri Bede*, pleads with sinner to repent so that they can inherit the kingdom of heaven. He further cautions that sinners who refuse to repent will pay for their sins in hell fire.

Ohwo or ru muemu weju muemu wo	–	Wicked ones repent.
Ihwo or chuji we juji vwo	–	Thieves, renounce stealing.
Me guono tota na kerieda	–	I want to tell witches and wizards
re vuri chochi. Wo vwi chochi	–	Wizards in the church. Don't
wo rui cover face. Komamọ	–	Hide under the church. Whatever
komamọ wo kore oye woche vu	–	You sow you shall reap.

Ofurie states here that only conversion can transform a wicked person, a thief, and a witch or wizard into a pious man. The song is didactic and it focuses on the virtue of morality.

Urhobo gospel music also serves as a vehicle for preaching the sermon. In some churches we visited as part of our fieldwork, we discovered that when songs are interjected in between sermons, members of the congregation are more attentive and it enjoins audience participation as it stirs body and soul to dance.

Amos Ighaka's *uyere* is synonymous with a sermon as shown below.

Ọghene rho wvo'ghogho	- God of Joy
Ọghene rho wve'sivwo	- God of healing
Jo'ghogho dia vwo k hwo	- Let happiness and joy
ri ke nyi ne na n	- Be with the listeners of this song
jo'ghogho dia kunu ro ka suine na	- Let joy be with the singer's mouth
re ve emo we vwo mrasa de	- So that your children
ku rhe rie vwo ga we fiki	- Can worship you and be
ri Jesu Kristi ro vwa vwa re ise	- Converted through Jesus Christ Amen

The importance of thanksgiving is also emphasized by Urhobo gospel singers. In *Uyere*, Amos Ighaka makes reference to the healing of ten lepers by Jesus in Luke 17:11-19. Among the ten healed lappers, only one came to show his gratitude to Jesus Christ. According to Ighaka, Jesus asked "where are the rest nine." Meaning:

Ohwo de ruemu ke vwe ke	- If somebody is kind to you
do da karovwe	- And you cannot appreciate his kind gesture, then you are ungrateful

He concludes that you should always give thanks to God for his infinite mercies.

Another gospel singer, Stephen Aruoture in "*Eka vi gbunu*" gives a vivid description of an Urhobo Christian overwhelmed with joy when he went to thank God after recovering from an accident. He states:

Oshare ovo re de vure	- There was once a man in the past
ro woma kprekede	- Who had a sudden injury
ode se de ro vwo kpevwo'ghene	- He fixed a date for thanksgiving.
ede na vwo tere evu ru wevwi ro"ghene	- In the church
oma vwo vwe ro share na	- Because the man was overwhelmed
orueha besie amua ke ba	- With joy, he never knew when
n'ehuroye ora rie	- The wrapper fell off his waist while he was engrossed in dancing.

Aruoture concludes that when God shows anyone his infinite mercy, he should always thank him.

Urhobo gospel music also has a therapeutic effect on the listeners since it has a healing effect and cools their nerves. In "Oghwefia" by Solomon Sharakure, the singer sooths the nerves of listeners by saying that God will extirpate evil from their midst.

Idebono ghwefia	- Devil, blow away.
Umuowora'kpo ghwefia,	- Evil deeds dissipate
avware r'emo r'oghene obo ta vware	- We are children of God. We are untouchable.
Ode ri Jesu ejo ghwe fia	- In the name of Jesus dissipate.
Avdware re mo r'oghene	- We are the children
Idebonoche se ru avware	- of God. The Devil
emo vuovo oghenefia	- Cannot do us any thing.

The singer hereby creates a sense of security for true believes in God and Jesus Christ.

A peculiar feature of recorded Urhobo gospel songs is Urhobo/English code mixing and code switching. This socio linguistic phenomenon is common in Urhobo land because the language is experiencing language shift. In "Igbunu ri de" Evang. Orogun, B. U. by there is an explicit example of code mixing and code switching below. It is good to be good. *Oshare ovo ero orue'se gaga*. (There was once a very kind man). He always does good to people. *Fiki ru'ruemu re esiri roye na* made to escape hire killer." A point worthy of note from the example of code mixing/code switching above is the level of literacy of some of the gospel singers. They are semi-literates. They use Banjo's variety ii of English. This variety is riddled with grammatical mistakes. It is pertinent to note here, however, that what matters is substance of these singers' message and not their level of education.

An important feature of music is its alliance with the physical movement called dance and Urhobo gospel music is not an exception in this regard. A major device used by Urhobo gospel singers to urge audience participation is inviting the listeners to clap and dance. In "Uyere," Amos Ighaka urges listeners to clap and sing thus:

Abo na abo chi chi	- Your hands, your hands, chi chi
wa te yabo k'oghene	- Clap for God.
we wor'agogo k'oghene	- Ring bell for God.
wa so, we gbe	- You should sing and dance.

This essay exhaustively examines the use and influence of Urhobo gospel music on the propagation of Christianity among the Urhobos. Urhobo gospel music serves as a vehicle for spreading the gospel. This brand of music also urges the Urhobo to renounce sin and materialistic life and imbibe a pious life. The music also emphasizes the importance of thanksgiving and it also has a therapeutic effect on the listener.

Works cited

Akpokodje, J. U. (2000) "The Urhobo People Language and Statehood," Unpublished Paper.
Aweto, B. (2002) "An Outline Geography of the Urhobo," Urhobo Language Society, Unpublished.
Aziza, R (1997) "Tone in Urhobo," PhD thesis, University of Ibadan, Ibadan.
Darah G. G. (1994) "The Image of the City in Urhobo Songs," Unpublished Paper.
Egbokhare, F. (2001) "The Nigerian Linguistic Ecology and the Changing Profile of Nigerian Pidgin," Igboanusi, H. (ed.) *Language Attitude and Language Conflict in West Africa*, Ibadan Enicrownfit Publishers.
Elugbe B. O. (1989) *Comparative Edoid: Phonology and Lexicon,* Port-Harcourt, University of Port-Harcourt Press.
Encyclopedia Britannica (1974) London, Helen Hemingway Benton Publisher.
Graham, B. (1989) *Ronnie Stern's Guide to Contemporary African Music* London, Pluto Press.
Otite, O. (1982): *The Urhobo People*. Ibadan, Heinemann Ed. Books.
Storey, J. (1996) *Cultural Studies and the Study of Popular Culture (Theories and Methods)* Edinburgh, Edinburgh University Press.

12

Praxis and aesthetics of Urhobo "disco" music

– *Sunny Awhefeada*

Culture is one of the most resilient features of any people. This is most illustrative among the Urhobo ethnic group of Nigeria. In spite of the pressure of change and the encroaching imperialistic culture, there are many indices that remain like denizens, which serve as indicators to certain peculiarities of the Urhobo. When these indicators are observed and analysed, one is confronted with Urhobo worldview and way of life, which embody its culture. Among these indicators of Urhobo culture is song or, more aptly put, music. And language, which is a people's most distinctive feature, is the vehicle of music.

The Urhobo are great composers, singers and performers. They superimpose several vignettes of their worldview and way of life on their composition and performance.

This essay will explore the praxis and aesthetics of Urhobo music with focus on two Urhobo minstrels, Johnson Adjan and Okpan Arhibo. Although there are many singers of Urhobo stock, the musical corpus of the duo has come to typify the matter and manner of contemporary Urhobo music. This music wears two unequal hats. The bigger of the two hats is indigenous while the other is foreign. The indigenous elements find expression in the minstrels' appropriation of the loric repertoire of Urhobo mostly through the indigenous language, the use of traditional musical instruments, nativist performance devices and costume among others. The foreign hat accommodates the deployment of modern musical equipments, the borrowing and sometimes corruption of foreign lexeme and so on.

Music is often described as poetry in motion. The dividing line between the two is tenuous and even nebulous. Thus, what goes for poetry goes for music. Both spring from emotion; the devices of imagery, tropes, repetition, sound, tone, mood, the architectonics and other elements that distinguish poetry from other modes of discourse are common to music. Urhobo music is not an exception to this. The appreciation of this will engender aesthetics. From the point of view of praxis, Urhobo music has many uses to which it can be put.

Beyond being functional as a means of entertainment, enlightenment and didactism, the genre can also serve other purposes, as this essay will reveal.

Like other art forms, Urhobo music reflects the social, economic and political temper of the time and place in which it is composed. An awareness of this provides the backcloth from which its praxis can be explored. Two musical albums, one by Adjan titled "Let them Say God is above" released in the early 1980s and the other by Okpan titled "Delta State Special" composed in the 1990s will be used as examples.

One very significant motif of Urhobo music that is foregrounded in both albums is the credo of the desirability of good over evil. This is a universalistic norm that has been demonstrated in the literature of other climes. In Adjan's album he intones that:

> Anyone that I have done good for, that is God's case, it is the case of heaven
> The only place I am thinking of that makes me not to be afraid.

While also philosophising on good and evil, Okpan croons thus:

> When my mother was alive, she cared for others' children. After she died her children roamed. Those that benefited from her, now pay back with evil.

The foregoing lines amble between philosophy and religion, the two concepts, which engender morality. Religion abhors evil and vivifies good, so does morality. The Urhobo worldview shares this concept. Adjan mentions God, good, heaven, evil, while Okpan mentions care, death, benefit, evil, these are lexical items that dominate religious injunctions and moral anecdotes.

Urhobo music has demonstrated a profound consciousness of its place, time and the burning issues of the day. In this sense one can describe this genre as a montage of social, political and economic issues. Adjan in his lines dons the garb of an apostle of public accountability. He protests with crusading gusto government's insensitivity to the plight of the masses. The lines aver that:

> Government, Nigeria's money. Let me know what happened to it school fees,
> Light bills, water bills.

The lines further reveal:

> Teacher's salaries are unpaid, workers are not paid... please pay the workers
> Dressing in spite of hunger is not good
> Come and see, hunger is bad for work
> The work done in hunger is not good

The children are always driven from school.

The foregoing lines adumbrate protest, a subtle, humanizing and regenerative kind of protest. In Okpan the trend veers into a lamentation of the economic woes of the masses:

> We can't buy Omo[1]
> Common salt we can't buy at all
> We can't buy tissue paper
> We can't buy matches
> Bread and sardine we can't buy.

The above lines portray the musicians as champions of the people's cause. In their enterprise can be found the people's plight.

The minstrels use their craft to promote relevant government policy thrust, engage in national discourse and social engineering by way of masses enlightenment. Adjan used his music to spread the gospel of Operation Feed the Nation (OFN). The OFN scheme was inaugurated in 1978 by General Olusegun Obasanjo, then a military head of state. The scheme was to encourage Nigerians in food production so that the country can be agriculturally self-reliant. Adjan sings that:

> The reigning Operation Feed the Nation
> My Friend you eat I eat
> Everybody should grow more food
> So that everybody can feed well.

The lines above will make a good piece of mass mobilization for government policy. The lines canvass support for the OFN by portraying its benefit. In the same breadth, Adjan delved into history to criticize the 1974 Udoji Award. In 1974, the government of General Yakubu Gowon instituted the Udoji awards during which government workers were paid huge sums of money. The award turned out to be a *faux pax* because of its many attendant negative consequences, one of which was inflation and impoverishment of non-governmental workers. Adjan says:

> The Udoji that was paid before
> It benefited some people while some did not benefit.

Lines such as the foregoing portray the minstrels as among the chronicles of their time.

In giving vent to the crowded chamber of history, the musicians appropriate some of the different political agitations of the homeland. One of such issues

---
[1] A brand of detergent

was the agitation for state creation in Nigeria. Since the late 1950s there have been several struggles for the creation of more regions and later states by groups that are dissatisfied with the status quo.

These agitations were the products of the tension arising from the obfuscating colonial arrangement where ethnic groups that were once autonomous were assembled into one entity. The people of the present Delta State for long agitated for its creation. Adjan, the quintessential minstrel joins in this agitation thus:

> The one Nigeria we are talking about...
> Some are enjoying while others are suffering
> Bendel is full of suffering
> Bendel is full of suffering
> Shehu Shagari if only you can create Delta for us.

These lines are redolent of the inequities in the Nigerian polity and the tension among once disparate people that are now lumped together by force. Having remonstrated the plight of his people, the minstrel goes on to cajole the influential men of power during the second republic (1979-1983). He avers:

> Shehu Shagari, I beg you with this song
> All of you in the Executive council
> I beg you with this song...
> Shagari, Alli, Ikpasa, Bolokor, Salubi.

The above is a plea to the political gladiators of the second republic who are now historical personages. In the second republic, Shagari was Nigeria's president, Alli was governor of the old Bendel State, Bolokor was a federal minister, Salubi was a commissioner while Ikpasa was a legislator.

A decade later, Okpan extended the thread, from where Adjan stopped to celebrate in song the creation of Delta State. In his song, Okpan celebrated the creation of the state and also eulogised the men of power at that time:

> The long awaited Delta State has been created bet it bring peace...
> Babangida, well done, Abacha well done Aikhomu well done...
> This is glory...o...

The characters, Babangida, Abacha and Aikhomu, all military officers formed the triumvirate that ruled Nigeria from 1985-1993 and then to 1998, a period when Delta State was created.

The singers' historical awareness is also thematized in Okpan's musical rendition of the electoral debacle of June 12 1993 and its consequences. In that election, the late M.K.O Abiola who won was denied victory by the ruling military cabal. Okpan captures the incidence thus:

> Papers were brought for voting

> After voting the winner is not declared
> Abiola said he won
> Urhobo believed that he won.

Okpan also portrays the ensuing inter-ethnic tension and social turmoil that greeted the annulment of the June 12 election as a section of the country interpreted it as grave injustice. Many people domiciled in states other than theirs relocated to their home states because of the looming signs of war. Some people died in the process as Okpan records:

> The Igbos ran home
> Lagos and Warri became quiet
> The war has not started
> But a lot of people are dead.

The above encapsulates the events of the period. Adjan on his own part, while exploring Nigerian history, re-echoes the tragedy of the Nigerian civil war (1967-1970) thus:

> Government the previous war
> The war was too disastrous.

History can thus be seen as a significant matter in Urhobo music.

Another preponderant issue in the pulsating rhythm of Urhobo music is that of cultural reclamation which is manifested in ethnic and linguistic pride. Hear Adjan:

> Urhobo are doing something that I dislike
> In Urhobo gathering they speak English that is a wrong habit
> I will sing with it...
> Come and see
> Let Urhobo garri be good for Urhobo (thrice)
> In Igbo gathering they speak Igbo
> In Yoruba gathering they speak Yoruba
> In Hausa gathering they speak Hausa
> But in Urhobo gathering they don't speak Urhobo.
> Come and see I can't deny my tribe.

The foregoing enunciates a cultural ethos while denouncing a people's deliberate deviation from their roots. Language is the most important element of one's identity, but most people who are ignorant of this, resort to speaking other languages to the detriment of theirs. This trend is popular among Urhobo youth and Adjan declaims against it. He sees in identifying with one's language an element of pride. Actions such as this can stem the tide of cultural imperialism.

Apart form the foregoing, Urhobo music serves other functions. The genre can be satirical and a means checking individuals and social excesses. It can also be a tool for setting personal scores. In this regard the musician fires verbal and abusive quills at his perceived traducers. Urhobo music is also a storehouse of wisdom, which manifests itself in the proverbs and anecdotes that the singer regales his audience with.

The music is also therapeutic. It soothes the buffetings and weariness of life and it is a veritable means of entertainment. Above all it is a source of enlightenment or education because the genre explores the people's cultural memory.

This exegesis has so far revolved round the praxis of Urhobo music. One will now comment on the aesthetics. Aesthetically, Urhobo music can be appreciated from two perspectives; auditory and visual. Sound and words are the most important ingredients of music. The symphony emanating from their synergy is pleasing to the ears. Apart from sound and words, there is the use of musical instruments, which add to the pleasantness of the echo.

There is also the opening and closing formula in Urhobo music as in loric performances. Here, the musician announces his presence, rouses his band of performers, dedicates the performance, greets the audience and says his intention.

At the end of the performance he greets the audience and performers, then rounds off.

Urhobo music appropriates several sound devices for different purposes. There is the use of repetition and parallelism. This accentuates the motif and aid the rhythmic flow of the song. The minstrel also engages the performers who form the chorus in the singing. The band of performers chants or re-echo the utterance of the minstrel to complement him and create a holistic lyric.

Urhobo music is rich in irony, hyperbole, proverbs, rhetorical questions, apostrophe, imagery and other devices that make it a tour de force in rhetorics.

In conclusion, from the point of view of visual appreciation, Urhobo music easily invites an audience to jig. Sometimes energetic, sometimes regal, depending on the beat, Urhobo dance steps are a spectacle to behold.

Note: The quoted lines are translations from Urhobo.

Works cited

Darah, G.G., "The image of the city in Urhobo songs," Unpublished Paper, 1994.
... "Social and Cultural Issues in the Exploration and Exploitation of Oil," Proceedings of the 1st Urhobo Economic Summit '98, Vol. 1, no 1 Nov.1999.
Graham, Ronnie, *Stern's Guide to Contemporary African Music*, London, Pluto Press, 1989.
Ojaide, Tanure, *Poetic Imagination in Black Africa*, North Carolina; Carolina Academic Press, 1996.
Roscoe, Adrian, *Uhuru's Fire: African Literature, East to South*, London; Cambridge University Press, 1977.
Storey, John, Cultural Studies and the Study of Popular Culture: Theories and Methods, Edinburgh; Edinburgh University Press, 1998.

13

The Urhobo orator and an occasion's experience

– *Tanure Ojaide*

Introduction

The Urhobo do value and honour communicators who also display oratorical skills. The Urhobo generally like someone with a strong personality, one who asserts himself, and exhibits leadership qualities associated with *Ivwri*, the power of defence and offence. To fulfil these goals, the person must possess communicative skills and special charm. The society and culture have carried this value of communication into the ceremonies and activities of the people.

From traditional times, the office and institution of the *ọtota* has been highly coveted and respected. Every traditional group discussion, family meeting, quarter's meeting, town's meeting, social associations and clubs, and others have an appointed *ọtota*. One is appointed for a quarter, village, town, or association. In other instances, he is either chosen or appointed for the group at the beginning of the meeting. The simplest of occasions, such as paying a visit to a friend, demands the use of an *ọtota*. Usually, the person next to the oldest in the group presents and accepts things on behalf of the group. That person is also an *ọtota*. However, this latter one is not a professional *ọtota*. While every person, especially male, can be an *ọtota*, there is the professional *ọtota* that is the origin of the new appellation of "Orator", still *ọtota* but with more than traditional responsibilities.

Also, a kingdom, like Agbon, has the title of *Ọtota* (a position currently held by Chief Patrick Bolokor), a role that approximates to that of a Prime Minister. In that position, he leads discussions at the palace and is generally regarded as next to the king in political power in the kingdom. So, the position of one speaking for and on behalf of a group or side has always been there in Urhobo history. This person is expected to have an effortless facility with words, rhetorical skills, acumen for making complex things simple, or obfuscating the wrongs of his side, and a good voice, among others. He is also expected to have a sense of the dramatic and know when to pause, what to emphasize, when to be humorous, and when to be sober. The "spokesperson" translation in English does not fully capture the totality of the work of the *ọtota* in traditional Urhobo society. He is in a sense the presenter and receiver of drinks and kola nuts and also the spokesman. The position carries great authority, as even the elders have to go through him to present a point of view.

The practice of *ọtota* is still very much alive. However, modernity has stretched it to mean more and less of the traditional term. From the oil boom days after the Nigerian Civil War (1967-70), many Urhobo imbibed social excesses that they used to attribute to Yoruba people. Lavish parties for one thing or the other, traditional marriages and western weddings, burials, installation of chiefs, and other socio-cultural occasions became avenues for display of affluence. Beginning randomly in the early 1970s and becoming increasingly acceptable as the norm by the early 1980s, a person (usually male) was invited or hired to serve as an "orator". The Urhobo orator is a post-modern *ọtota*, combining some of the known qualities of an orator in the true sense of the word and those of the traditional *ọtota*. Even though the Nigerian economy has had a downturn in recent years, the practice of orator has already been so embedded in the society that it has become an integral part of a celebration. Failure to provide an orator means that the ceremony is incomplete and could lead to snide comments that question the preparedness of the celebrants for the occasion.

The mere fact that the English term "orator" is used universally among the educated, rather than the Urhobo *ọtota*, tells its post-modern status. With Western education taken seriously by the Urhobo from the beginning of colonial times, many educated Urhobo must have studied some Shakespeare at least at the secondary school level. *Julius Caesar* has been a classic text in Nigerian secondary schools and the notion of the orator apparently derives from Mark Anthony's speech turning the crowd/mob against the conspirators who killed his master. His famous speech of "I come to bury Caesar and not to praise him" reverberates on most students' lips.

Origin and development

The practical origin of the Urhobo orator, as different from the traditional already mentioned, can be traced to inter-house sports competitions in schools around. The headmaster or principal used to invite an announcer to such occasions. This announcer was not paid but given refreshment. When S. A. Ofua started, he did it as free work that he so much relished and to promote himself.

He was basically an announcer and a master of ceremony, who interspersed his announcements of the events with proverbs and humorous anecdotes. He formed a small group of acrobats who entertained as he talked, especially at intervals. He was a favourite guest at inter-house sports and at Independence Day (October 1) and Children's Day (May 27) celebrations.

The *ọtota*/orator genre is so dynamic that it grew from one man's pastime to an established institution. Ofua later abandoned the acrobatic side and constituted another group, a sort of chorus, to help him sing and dance as he announces proceedings of the events. He, thus, reinforced the entertainment side of his role at these occasions. He started to appear in more than school and government functions in traditional ceremonies. Both S. A. Ofua and Emọjevu Echero started about the same time in the late 1960s and performed at inter-house sports competitions before moving to traditional ceremonies and social events. Miller Agbuna of Orhokpor, who lived at Okpara Inland, was also a pioneer orator.

With the explosion of orators, there arose the need for an association to regulate the profession's work. The first association of orators was formed at Ughelli, and it was headed by Emọjevu Echero. Then came the Agbarho group formed at the behest of Power Onojete. Later Onojete and Ofua formed an Agbon association of orators with Ofua as chairman, Agbuna as vice chairman, and Onojete as secretary.

With many clan-based associations in existence, a need arose for a national association of Urhobo orators. A meeting was summoned to Ofua's home at Oviorie for a conference. All the known local associations and practicing "orators" were invited, including Ukoko Onogbo, a teacher in Sapele. Unlike other associations that turned up en mass, the Ughelli association only sent a delegation and did not show much interest in the national body. In any case, a national body of Urhobo *ọtotas*/orators was formed with Ofua as president general, Echero first vice president, Agbuna second vice president, and Onojete secretary general. The national association adopted a constitution and had its rules.

Division came to the association when Gamaliel Onosode declared his intention to contest for the presidency of Nigeria in the mid-1990s. At a meeting at the Petroleum Training Institute, Effurun, accusations of mismanagement of the national association's funds were levied against some officials. Many of the orators dropped their membership of the national body and formed a rival national association that elected Echero as president general. The Echero camp is now the official body formally registered with Delta State government as *Ukoko r'Etota r'Urhobo* (National Association of Urhobo Professional Orators). This group suspended Ofua, who holds to his camp.

The major objective of the orators is reflected in the Ughelli branch's motto of "Uruemu Urhobo! *Ayoro ga*! (Urhobo culture! It must be maintained!). It is the orators with Ofua as a principal person that formed the Urhobo Anthem, which runs as follows:

> Ko ko ko ogbare
> Urhobo eeh! Orere r'ivie san.
> Ko ko ko ogbare
> Urhobo eeh! Orere r'ivie san.
> Obo r'Urhobo jevwe na
> Orho ofan jevwe otioye-en
> Ede ofa me ch'akpo
> Oto r'Urhobo me wan rhe-o
> Urhobo eeh! Orere r'ivie san.
> Arioma-oo

Many orators ask the assembled crowd to rise and either sing or play the Urhobo Anthem at the commencement of celebrations. I have personally experienced this as Ofua and his group sang it at Orhuwherun on May 12, 2001 when I hired him to perform during my "condolence visit" to my wife and her family on the death of my mother-in-law.

The orators want to preserve the language and make it grow with the times. They, thus, have the prime objective of maintaining the culture in all its ramifications. They educate the populace on the traditions and their changing with modernity. With the anthem, they stir up Urhobo nationalism and promote Urhobo unity and interests in the multi-ethnic Nigerian federation.

Education, training and preparations

The Urhobo orator invited or hired to perform on social occasions, therefore, is a fairly educated person. Many have secondary school education, some dropped out and others completed. Many others, including Achanacho and Obireri, are graduates and one (Onojete) has a doctoral degree. The minimum qualification though is a primary school education and much life experience. The orator cannot perform his role successfully if he were an illiterate person. He must be at least a little enlightened, but not necessarily much, to perform his duties. He assumes a position of importance and authority in cultural settings everywhere. Most of them are teachers in the elementary school, secondary school, and one (Dr Onojete) in the university.

There is no formal training for the orator. With talent, a little Western education and much knowledge of Urhobo language and folklore, he improves through practice. Apart from Ofua, Echero, and Agbuna from whom many of these orators learnt their skills, most first attend occasions and listen to older orators and then start their own careers. One can talk of three generations of Urhobo orators up to now.

The pioneer orators are Ofua, Echero, and Agbuna. The second generation of orators apprenticed under the three major pioneers, especially Ofua. The major figures of the second generation are Raphael Okejepha Achanacho of Okpara, Power Onojete of Ovu, and David Akperhe of Olomu (but lives at Ughelli). The third generation of orators learnt their trade from their immediate elders. Tisio of Agbarho is disciple of Onojete, as Tisio of Oviorie (Peter Palmer) and Agadaye Omuofa are disciples of Achanacho.

Each individual must weigh whether or not he has the talent that the position demands. He must be able to invent anecdotes effortlessly and ex-tempore and thus possess an agility of mind and resourcefulness. He should have such mastery of the Urhobo language that he can criticize subtly even as he praises. The orator is really a poet, singer, performer, rhetorician, and entertainer all in one. He has to be skilled in so many entertaining/performance areas as to keep an occasion exciting and lively enough for him to be reciprocated with lavish donations or "spraying".[1]

Once one has made up one's mind on becoming an orator, there is the procurement of the equipment for the job. A loudspeaker and relevant tools are acquired. Those that sing and play music have to procure the relevant instruments. Most of the orators dress in a smart traditional Urhobo way - a wrapper, a shirt, a cap, a walking stick, and a necklace of coral beads or gold. He could be formal, as described, or informal. I have seen several orators dressed casually, one with a French suit at a night burial ceremony.

The orator is hired and his fame, based on earlier performance rating, affects his demand. On the special occasion in which he is to perform, he goes early to survey the venue of the occasion and select a strategic position for his performance. This could be a day or two before the actual date of the occasion. He is usually given a central location. On the very day, he goes early and sets up his equipment under his canopy in the apportioned position. He is given a central place because he has to reach everybody. He tests his equipment and makes sure everything is fine before the occasion starts.

Performance fees

The orator lives on what he is paid in his regular job or work, the fee he charges to perform, and the money "sprayed" on him by celebrants and spectators at the occasion. What started as free or volunteer work in primary and secondary schools athletic competitions with time turned to a fee-charging profession. As the orators moved from manning public address systems to entertain and do other things on social occasions, they started to ask for pay. After all, they had to

---

[1] "Spraying" is the act of literally and publicly showering a dancer or performer with money, usually associated with the affluent or those seeking notice and social recognition. Spraying has, however, gained wider practice and less opprobrium.

buy their equipment and pay transportation costs. With many principals of secondary schools without the necessary vote to pay them, the orators were not satisfied with mere refreshments of soft drinks and perhaps crackers. They started to appear less and less at inter-house sports and more at the traditional burials and marriages. Usually, a man paying a condolence visit to his parents-in-laws seeks the services of an orator. The orator is also sought to perform at the burial ceremony proper.

As of now, the fee to engage an orator falls between two and twenty thousand naira depending upon his status in the profession. The young ones, who want to be known, charge very little. Such orators look for posters announcing deaths, marriages, or other occasions and approach the celebrants to render their services. These ones ask for fees to pay for their instruments and transportation costs and rely on the money they would be "sprayed" during the occasion. Others charge according to the wealth of the celebrant. If the celebrant happened to be a friend or family person, the orator would charge less or just ask to be paid whatever amount was reasonable. Ofua, doubtless the most senior orator, charges between twenty thousand and thirty thousand naira for an occasion. Dr Onojete charges between eight and twelve thousand naira. In an interview, he told me he had charged twenty thousand naira for a session in distant Port Harcourt.

The orator may have another avenue for making money - as said earlier, most are teachers in elementary or secondary schools - but takes his profession seriously. In fact, it is now the full-time occupation of many like Ofua. An occasion, ceremony, or party is not complete without the orator. In some parties, those who attended remember more the orator than any other thing that took place. That is why the celebrant will pay what is needed to retain his services.

Related African traditions

The Urhobo are not the only ones to have this practice in Africa. Two bardic traditions easily come to mind: the *griot* in West Africa and the *imbongo* of the Zulu and Xhosa of South Africa. In the Senegambian region and the neighbouring Mali and Guinea areas, the *griot* has been a professional poet and entertainer from the beginning. He lives on what he is given and sings praises of those who lavish money on him. In fact, there is a saying that the *griot*'s tongue becomes smoother with gifts. Like the *ǫtota* in recent Urhobo history, the *griot* is not only a poet but also an entertainer and more. He is a chronicler, who is supposed to memorize the lineage of kingship and the unwritten laws and constitution of his people. Put simply, he is the custodian of the culture, a role the Urhobo *ǫtota* as the one to be discussed, emphasizes is his to carry out.

In South Africa, the Zulu and Xhosa people have their *imbongi*, poets who entertain at public occasions. Both Trevor Cope and Jeff Opland have written extensively on these performers of *izibongo*. They are mainly praise singers who entertain at public occasions and weave the most elaborate of praises to lavish on guests or their hosts. Again, the freer one gives them money, the freer they lavish praises on you. However, as a result of clan history and praise names, the *imbongi* has specific allusions to borrow from and there are certain formulas in the praise convention to adhere to. While the Zulu *imbongi* is mainly a memoriser who recites what he has earlier composed or passed on to him, the Xhosa *imbongi* composes poetry in performance - a unique feat which David Manisi has shown in recent times in his South Africa and outside in visits to the United States.

The Urhobo *otota* or orator combines the traditions of both the Zulu and Xhosa *imbongi* because at some times he recites what he has memorised and at other times he composes as he performs. The aim of this seeming digression to other traditions is to show the antecedents of the Urhobo orator and other related traditions in Africa.

The orator tradition: Ijono Akpeje's performance

One can say at this juncture that contemporary Urhobo life requires the orator on occasions of celebrations, traditional marriages and weddings, burials, and other parties. Urhobo burials of old and successful people are not occasions for grief but of celebration, which the orator comes to accentuate with his thrilling performance. He is at such a social occasion meant for cultural affirmation and validation.

He starts to perform as celebrants and guests arrive. At this time, he praises the celebrants and keeps waiting people from being bored or too impatient about the starting time. With Urhobo people generally not keeping to time and not being punctual, impatient people who could have gone away stay to listen to the orators.

On Saturday, March 29, 2003, I observed an Urhobo orator, Ijono Akpeje of Okwagbe, at a traditional bride-price paying/traditional marriage ceremony at Owhawha in Ughelli South local government of Delta State (Nigeria). It was on the occasion of the traditional marriage of Emmanuel London Ubuara and his wife, Florence Oghenemuodeowho Aluya. I arrived at the right time. The woman's family elders were hosts of the occasion and were about to welcome their guests, Mr. Ubuara and his family and friends, to Owhawha. It is from this observation that I write this about the Urhobo orator.

The Urhobo orator fills in gaps outside official deliberations. At the time of the presentation and acceptance of kola nuts and drinks, the orator keeps quiet. The two families have their own traditional *ọtota*s and were those involved in the welcoming rites. The hired orator knows when it is his time to talk or perform. At some points, if he appears carried away and silence is demanded, one of the hosts will ask him to stop to allow the audience to turn attention to the major event. After the acceptance of kola nuts and drinks, they are served round. At this time that hosts and guests are occupied with drinking and sharing kola nuts, the orator performs.

He starts with a very humorous anecdote to attract people's attention and to cause laughter. The orator, on this occasion, first pours praises on the chief celebrant, Emmanuel London Ubuara, and his people of Ekakpamre. Since he is from Okwagbe, he praises Ekakpamre and Okwagbe as the towns that have coal tar and light in Ujevwe Kingdom, a half-truth but a statement that makes Mr. Ubuara and his family happy. The orator announces the presence and entrance of dignitaries at the occasion. A certain ex-local government chairman appears and is recognized with fanfare. The politician that he is, he waves his fly-whisk, and "sprays" some naira notes on the orator who pours encomiums on him to boost his ego.

This orator, a product of the highly patriarchal Urhobo society, makes many chauvinistic statements, which the men enjoy at the expense of the so many women present. He says women that wear trousers have one leg in their marriage and the other outside. He also says that women that drink beer from a bottle are bad. Of course, the orator carries the values, belief systems, and world-view of his people. This particular one is not sensitive enough to shed chauvinistic ideas. He lauds women that call their husbands "my lord" or "my heart." To him, for a woman to call her husband "Papa Tega" or "Daddy" is not romantic enough. Interestingly, he does not talk about how men should address or call their wives.

At a stage the two families involved in the marriage, Iseri and Kengben, went into the sitting room of the adjoining house to complete the rites of traditional marriage. This is the time that the orator is allowed free range to entertain. However, on this occasion, as in others I have witnessed, he competes for attention with the hired musicians who also want to entertain. A gospel music group is in attendance. They start to sing and dance to church songs amidst intermittent interruptions from the orator. The orator introduces more dignitaries around with praises.

At a time both Mr. Emmanuel Ubuara and his senior brother come to "spray" the orator money and he falls into a trance of encomiums. The senior brother, Frank, works for the Schlumberger company. The orator, seeing the crisp and neat twenty naira notes being "sprayed" on him, observes that the notes smell of Schlumberger. He says that the smell of new naira notes drives roaches from a house. This is the contrast with notes soiled with dirty hands handling ice fish, meat, and other dirty professions. He is very hard on poverty in an environment that shows palpable signs of malnutrition among the children and adults.

The orator also praises the man for his past charitable giving and makes him a role model of men. To please the bridegroom, he invents the most liberal epithets to describe his generosity, his kindness, his dignity, and his leadership qualities. He engages in rhetoric saying, "London, your name fits you; London, you shine above everybody else; London you are the rich the rich go to borrow from; London, the man every woman would like to be her husband." The major areas he talks about are women and wealth. He condemns liberated women as hard as he condemns and ridicules the poor.

The orator serves as one who understands the culture and, aware that others may not know, fills in the gaps. He interprets the symbolism of some rites. For instance, he explains the ritual significance of the family meeting and the man and the woman drinking from one glass of gin that the elders have prayed over. He, thus, has cultural knowledge, which he conveys to the audience.

The orator takes a break as he takes his food and drinks. The celebrants make sure that he is adequately served so that he will be pleased to perform his best. This break takes about twenty minutes; time the music group fully uses. After refuelling, the orator in the second phase of his performance tells a barrage of anecdotes that sends the people reeling with laughter. Many of these are bawdy or vulgar tales. He tells of a town-bred five-year old that his parents took to spend a few days with his grandfather in the village. The grandfather, an elderly man, dressed in work rags, set out to clear the grass around his house. As he bent down, his testicles came out dangling. The young boy shouted, "Grand Daddy, see juju!" The old man stood, baffled, and told the boy there was no juju around. This went on two more times and the next time the old man told him, "If you see juju again, hold it!" And as the man bent down and the testicles dangled again, the innocent boy dived to hold them and told him, "See the juju." The old man laughed hilariously with his brownish teeth and said, "No, this is not juju. It is from here that you came to life!"

Another anecdote that caught my fancy shows the orator's education. I have no doubt in my mind that he borrowed this from Chinua Achebe's *No Longer at Ease*. He tells of a girl who was called for an interview for a job. She was asked so many questions, which she answered well. Then she was reminded that in the form she filled, she omitted "Sex" and she said "Three times a night!" The interviewers asked her to go and that she would hear from them later. This, to me, appears to be an exaggeration or distortion of Achebe's female character that says "Twice a week!"

It is important to put in context the use of bawdy or vulgar jokes. Many of these ceremonies, especially traditional marriage and burials, are avenues for flirtations. Many men and women, young and old, seem to have flirtation in mind while going to attend them. For long kept down by patriarchal norms, Urhobo women in modern times see these ceremonies as liberating avenues where they can release themselves emotionally. The orators are aware of this libidinal desire and play to the men and women's fantasies.

Socio-cultural importance of the orator

The orators are not mere entertainers. They serve as custodians of not only the culture and language but also as satirists of the mores of the society. For instance, the anecdotes described have their moral and ethical dimensions. But significantly, the orators desire to uphold cultural values they feel are being violated. Depending on the occasion, an orator emphasizes some ills of the society. They deal with gender issues, especially women straying from traditional norms of the patriarchal society. They also satirize corrupt politicians, who embezzle the commonwealth's money out of greed. They also hit hard materially minded and hypocritical religious leaders and their groups. They are against all forms of deviants so as to keep everybody in line and thereby maintain a healthy cultural ethos. They, thus, have a didactic side in addition to the entertainment.

Multi-talented personality

In-between anecdotes and stories of humour, the orator sings and dances. This shows his all-round nature as a composite entertainer and performer. He is smart and exhibitionist about his own dressing. In a few cases, the orator has a music and dance group as Ofua does. They have their music taped in cassettes, which they make available for interested people to buy. However, the orator whose performance is being discussed has no musical group.

After the groom and bride emerge from the family house, an indication that they have been pronounced husband and wife by the elders, the orator announces that they will take their seats of honour already prepared under a special canopy adorned with red, pink, and blue ribbons and balloons. He takes on the role of a master of ceremony and announces that a single file should be formed as people dance to the music of the gospel group and go to offer their gifts and "spray" the two chief celebrants. He has a keen eye on what is happening and is quick to speak over the music when he notices an individual "spraying" so much money.

The orator position is doing much to revitalize the Urhobo language. At every occasion possible, he uses proverbs and axioms to express his ideas and feelings. To this orator, the traditional eldest woman of the town or village ("*oni ewheya*") wears no bra. He also says the eldest man in the community does not beat the gong - in other words, he cannot be the town-crier. He uses and invents praise names such as "The woman looking for money"; "Rain that falls on a rock"; and, "Gogorogo" to which he responds respectively. No doubt, he has facility for words and at no time does he fall short of expressions or fail to entertain. He makes allusions to local politics. A certain Ogboru came, and, bearing in mind Great Ovedje Ogboru, the Alliance for Democracy's candidate for governor in Delta State, states that "This is our Ogboru, Michael; not Great whose greatness we are yet to see." His partisan political stand affects his comments. In any case, he draws laughter and so succeeds in his oratorical call.

Cognizant of the fact that some, if not many, of those in attendance do not speak or understand Urhobo, he speaks English now and then. Many times, he mixes Urhobo and English. While this is meant to entertain, it occasionally reflects his level of education. When he delves into English, he is bombastic and falls into malapropisms. Nobody around really cares about his mistakes and everybody roars to his satisfaction.

Conclusion

The Urhobo orator tradition is relatively new and still evolving. Currently, in its third generation, it has become an integral part of Urhobo social life that one expects at major ceremonies. Only a men-only profession now, there is no reason why women should not take to it. This is necessary to counter the overwhelming male chauvinism displayed. Also the orators should be more sensitive to the underprivileged in society and not just praise the rich, many of whom are corrupt and got their wealth at the expense of the common people. While the entertainment teaches pleasurably now, there are more avenues to be explored to make the education more humane and learned. It is a major avenue to reach so many and the responsibility should be such that the orator should be a cultural role model for the Urhobo people.

The orator shows how Urhobo culture is dynamically adjusting to contemporary life and bringing fresh air to an old tradition. The mere fact that the "orator" appears in traditional ceremonies of marriage, burials, or installations shows how the Urhobo people, while being modern and postmodern, retain their cultural identity and are proud of it.

Works cited and references

Niane, D.T., ed., *Sundiata,* Harlow: Longman, 1979.
Opland, Jeff, *Xhosa Oral Poetry: Aspects of a Black South African Tradition,* Johannesburg: Ravan, 1983.
-----------, *Xhosa Poets and Poetry*, Cape Town: David Philip Publishers, 1998.
Otite, Onigu (ed), *The Urhobo People*, Ibadan: Heinemann, 1983.

14

Teaching the word across languages: the Christian gospel and evangelisation in Urhobo

– *Sunny Awhefeada*

Language is humanity's primary means of communication. Over the years, explorations and discoveries have enabled and still enable mankind to discover more people who have their different and distinctive language entities. The biblical story of the Tower of Babel tells us about the origin of different languages. Going by this story, God descended different languages on men so that their plan of building a tower bound for heaven would come to naught. It is an inexplicable irony that the humanity, which God dispersed by endowing it with plural languages, is today angling towards being united by God's message and promise of salvation through the various languages with which God dispersed it.

One of Jesus Christ's last injunctions to his disciples as recorded in the Gospels, according to Matthew 28:19 and Mark 16:15, was that they should go and make disciples from every nation on earth. Looking back to two thousand years ago and now, one can conclude that the realization of that injunction is on the ascent. And language is the tool with which it is being realized.

The advent of European explorers and traders in the Niger Delta dates back to 1472 with the arrival of the Portuguese. The "first white men" were not missionaries; rather they were merchants. Obaro Ikime (1965) argues that though the first arrivals were Christian, their efforts at Christianisation were not serious. It was early in the twentieth century that the first missionaries reached Urhoboland. M.Y. Nabofa (1980:232) posits that radical changes in the religious beliefs of the people started taking place since about 1900. Thus, the first groups of missionaries to reach the Urhobo at that time, according to S.U. Erivwo (1991:82-84), were the Niger Delta Pastorate (WDP), the Church Missionary Society (CMS), and then the Catholic Church. These "fishers of men" cast their nets and got native converts who attended their churches and whose children attended newly established missionary schools.

In order to propagate the gospel, the early missionaries taught their converts and particularly their children the rudiments of the English language to aid their evangelising mission. Some of the converts having been endowed with the "new" language became tools for spreading the gospel of the "new" religion in their mother tongue.

The foregoing explains the origin of gospel preaching in the Urhobo language. One hundred years after, the phenomenon is still strong as there is still a felt need to spread the gospel in indigenous languages. Thus, many churches in Urhoboland, especially in the villages still use the Urhobo language as their medium of evangelisation. While some churches in the urban centres use the language for interpretation, the English language is unintelligible to most rural dwellers. This makes the use of Urhobo during church services in rural areas inevitable. In places like Orogun, Kokori, Evwreni, Uwherun, Ekakpamre, and Okpara, most of the churches use Urhobo as the medium of communication. In urban settlements such as Ughelli, Warri, and Sapele, where the flock is a mix of people with different linguistic backgrounds, some of the churches have different services in which Urhobo is used or on the other hand some engage the use of Urhobo interpreters. This is necessary in order that the gospel would be heard and grasped by all. Allied with this is the pride which delivering the gospel in Urhobo will invest on the people. This is very important, because as R. O. Aziza (1999: 50) observes, language is a measure of a people's identity and pride.

There is nothing that is characteristically different between the gospel in Urhobo and the one in English apart from the lack of intelligibility between the two languages. The content and message of the gospel in both languages are similar. The same goes for the form and rhetorical strategies. The content of the sermon in both languages normally derives from the Holy Bible, the Christian book of worship.

The writer deliberately visited two different churches to study the use of Urhobo in the service and propagation of the Christian message. The sermons delivered in Urhobo in two different churches revolve round the questions of sin (*umuemu*), confession (*omefan*), forgiveness (*eghovwon*), salvation (*arhon*), holy living (*akpo ofuanfon*), humility (*oma evwokpoto*), peace and well being (*ufuoma*), and blessing (*ebruvwiyo*). There are also the issues of tribulations (*okpetu/ukpokpoma*), poverty (*obevwen*), witchcraft (*orhan*), barrenness (*egan*), and illness (*emiavwen*) among others.

Both sermons began with prayers after the preachers said in Urhobo, "*we dja ne erhowo*" meaning "let us pray". In both prayers the preachers called on God (*Oghene*) to speak (*tota*) through the preachers (*owhowheta ro ghene*) and to help the listeners (ihworikeron) to hear well and abide by what would be preached. The preachers referred flock to the source of the sermons, which are the biblical books of Jeremiah, Chapter 31 and Hebrews, Chapter 5 respectively. They read the texts in Urhobo, explained them and also chose instances from daily experience to buttress the messages.

The message from the book of Jeremiah dwells on the tribulation of the children of God and his promise of redemption which would bring them joy, abundance and fulfilment. The preacher likened the foregoing to contemporary tribulation (*ukpokpoma*) and urged the flock (*igegede*) to carry out acts of confession (*omefan*) and repentance (*obo ekworherie*) so that God's promised salvation (*arhon*) can be theirs. He advised the congregation (*ukoko*) to be humble (*omakpotọ*) so that God can have pity (*ohore*) on them and give them his grace (*esiri*). He edified them that their fight against poverty (*obevwen*), witchcraft (*oran*), childlessness (*egan*), illness (*emianvwen*) would be over as soon as they repent and believe (*segbuyota*) in God. He acknowledged the existence of enemies (*ivwighren*) and proclaimed that the fire (*erharen*) of God would consume them. He consoled the congregation that victory (*ovwikparobo*) and happiness (*omavwerhovwen*) would soon be theirs.

The other sermon from the book of Hebrews centres on steadfastness (*emudiagan*). It emphasises the role of the priest (*oriren*) as an intermediary between God and man. He is there to prevent those who are ignorant (*irijeriente*) from going astray (*eyan ghwre*). The message is to encourage the followers (*idibo*) or the faithfuls (*evwata*). It also dwells on sacrifices (*izobo*), prayers (*erhovwon*), submission and obedience (*oma evwokpoto*).

In ordinary conversation among most Urhobo there is the tendency to infuse English lexical items such as "but", "because", "look", "table", or strings of English words. But it is significant to say that both preachers did not use English words or expressions throughout the period the sermons lasted. There are inventions or substitutes for all the English words so that the Urhobo words collocate effectively. Words such as chapter and verse are translated as "*uyovwi*" meaning head and "*owo*" meaning leg. The logic of this is that as chapter precedes verse so does head precedes leg. The names of people and places in the Bible however remain unchanged but pronounced in an Urhobo accent.

In the course of the sermon, there were gospel songs in Urhobo to further elucidate the message and alleviate the boredom of sermonizing. The preachers appropriated some rhetorical techniques such as repetition, exaggeration, humour, rhetorical questions, proverbs, anecdotes and gestures for the purpose of emphasis and driving home the points being made. Most significantly, the diction of the preachers was simple and unambiguous.

Language, this essay submits at the beginning, is man's most significant means of communication. Without the gospel being translated into many languages in which it now lives, majority of the world's population would not have known about it. If this had not been so, the biblical injunctions, hinted at early in this treatise, would not have been realized. Also the various manifestations of the gospel to mankind would not have reached those people outside the area in which the language the gospel was originally conceived and written. But thanks to the studious efforts of linguists and translators and the untiring zeal of missionaries the language barrier to communication has in many ways been broken. Teaching the world (of God) across languages has found a testament in the Christian gospel in Urhobo.

Works cited

Aziza, R.O., "The Role of Language in the Development of the Urhobo Nation," *Proceedings of the 1ˢᵗ Urhobo Economic Summit 98,* Vol.1 No 1 November 1999.
Erivwo, S.U., *Traditional Religion and Christianity in Nigeria: The Urhobo People,* Ekpoma: Dept. of Religious Studies and Philosophy, 1991.
Ikime, Obaro, "The Coming of the CMS into the Itsekiri, Urhobo and Isoko Country," *Nigeria Magazine* September 1965.
Nabofa, M.Y., "Igbe Religious Movements," in Onigu Otite, ed., *The Urhobo People,* Ibadan; Heinemann, 1980.
The Holy Bible: New International Version.

Index

Abacha, Gen Sani; 136
Abi; 6
Abiola, M.K.O.; 136
Abraka; 83, 86, 96, 100, 106
Achanacho, Raphael O.; 16, 142
Adjan, Johnson; 16, 133-137
Adjective qualifiers; 45
Adjectives; 41
Adjekota; 98
Adverbs; 50
Afiesere; 98
Aganbi; 13
Agbarha; 95, 101
Agbarha-Ame; 95
Agbarho dialect; 15
Agbarho; 6, 83, 95, 101, 102
Agbon; 6, 13, 83, 84, 95, 97, 100, 101, 139
Agboro, Francis; 1
Agbuna, Miller, of Orokpor; 141, 142
Ahwinahwin, of Ughelli; 13
Aikhomu, Admiral; 136
Akindele, Femi and Adegbite, Wale; 57, 99, 102, 103
Akpeje, Ijono; 145
Akperhe, David; 143
Akpokodje, J.U.; 131
Aluya, Florence O.; 145
Amraibure; 14
Ancient Urhobo; 7
Appiah, K.; 121, 125
Apple and Muysken; 57
Approximants; 69
Arhavwarien; 95, 100, 101
Aruoture; Stephen; 130
Asaba; 14, 15
Asorbed Portuguese words; 11
Atamu Social Club; 16, 109
Ativie, K.; viii, ix, 55
Avwraka (Abraka); 95, 98
Aweto, B.; 127, 131
Awhefeada, S.; viii, ix, 133, 151
Awoonor, Kofi; 19

Aziza, R., iii, viii, ix, 2, 16, 19-21, 31, 63, 75, 82, 109, 128, 131, 152, 154
Babangida, Gen.; 136
Barber, C.L.; 85,
Berger, P.L.; 119, 125
Bini (Benin); 84, 97, 98, 100, 106
Bolokor, Chief Patrick; 136, 139
CCV syllable; 80
Chinua Achebe; 147
Christian gospel music and evangelisation in Urhobo; 151
Church Missionary Society (CMS); 151
Code switching; 56
Code-mixing; 55
 - sociolinguistic phenomenon; 60
Colour adjectives; 34
Complete Urhobo Bible; 13
Conjunctions; 52
Consonant segments; 64
Cope, Trevor; 144
Cultural Policy for Nigeria (1988); 105
CV syllable; 80
Darah, G.G.; viii, ix, 2, 12, 13, 16, 19, 96, 103, 105, 131, 138
De-adjectival class nouns; 35
Degema; 75
Deverbal nouns; 36
Dictionary of Urhobo language; 17
Diop, Cheikh Anta; 3, 19
Ebiegberi, Alagoa; 19
Echero, Omojevu; 141-143
Edjophe; 13
Edoid (Pan-Edo); 4, 5, 21, 70, 75, 127, 128
Effurun; 18, 86, 106, 108, 128, 141
Egbokhare, F.; 127, 131
Eghwu; 95, 97-102
Eguono Club; 16
Ekakpamre; 146, 152
Ekeh, Peter; 2
Eku; 13, 114
Elugbe, B.O.; 19, 32, 70, 75, 82, 127, 128

Emedo, T.; 12
Epha; 7
Ephron-Oto; 95, 99
Erhirhi, Chief J.; 109
Erivwo, S.U.; 7, 96, 103, 151, 154
Eruwa; 128
Essien; 61
Eta Urhobo magazine; 17
Evolution of names; 14
Evolution of Urhobo language; 1
Evwreni; 95, 97, 152
Ewu; 15
Exclamations; 52
Ferguson, C.A.; 92
Foss, Perkins; 2
Fricatives; 66
Functions of tone in Urhobo; 21
Genitival constructions in Urhobo; 45
Glide formation; 74
Goldsmith, J.; 32
Government communication/language policies, impact of; 14
Gowon, General Yakubu; 135
Graham, B.; 131
Graham, Ronnie; 138
Grammar of code-mixing in Urhobo; 57
Grammatical tones; 25
Great Bantu Migration; 3
Griot; 144
Gyekye, K.; 121, 125
Haggard, T.; 125
Haughen, E.; 103
Holliday, M.A.K.; 53
Holmes; 60
Hotel de Jordan; 14
Hountondji, P.; 121, 125
Ibori, Governor; 108
Idjerhe; 95, 100
Igala; 4
Igboze; 97
Ighaka, Amos; 129, 131
Ijo (Izon, Ijaw); 5-7, 56, 83, 84, 100, 101, 109, 127
Ikime, Obaro; 20, 151, 154
Internal poetic dynamics; 13
International Labour Organisation; 106
Ise; 14

Ishan; 4
Isoko; 5, 6, 9, 56, 83, 97, 100, 109, 128
Ite; 14
Itsekiri; 5-7, 9, 56, 84, 100, 110
Ivwri; 14
Iwe, Agori; 1
Iwhrekan; 13
Izibongo; 145
Jenkins; William; 99
Jike, V.T.; viii, ix, 119
Jung, G.C.; 124, 125
Kamwangamalu, N.M.; 57
Kelly, J.; 32, 82, 103
Khosa; 144, 145
Kokori; 14, 83, 86, 152
Kwa font (languages); 17; 120, 126
Language and loss of identity; 108
Languages in contact; 56
Lexical tones; 22
Lexis and structure in Urhobo; 33
Likibe; 128
Locative adverbs; 35
Malmkjaer, K.; 103
Masolo, D.A.; 121
Mbiti, J.S.; 121, 125
Memerume; 13
Modernity and urbanization, impact of; 15
Mowarin, M.; viii, ix, 127
Mukoro, Mowoe; 13, 16
Murray, Jocelyn; 4
Nabofa; N.Y.; 96, 97, 103, 124, 151, 154
Naming of divination; 7
Nasals; 68
National Association of Urhobo Professional Orators; 141
Negation and interrogation; 29
Niane, D.T.; 149
Nicholas, Ralph; 99
Niger Delta Pastorate; 151
Niger-Kordofan group of language; 4
Nominalizations; 38
Numbering method; 86
Nyasani, J.M.; 121
Obasanjo, General Olusegun; 135
Obiaruku; 6
Obiomah, Daniel; 1

Obireri; 142
Odova; 14
Ofodidun; 12
Ofua, S. A.; 16, 86, 92, 139, 140-144, 148
Ofurie, singer; 129
Ogbariemu, Chief Dozen; 3, 4, 7
Ogboru, Great Ovedje; 149
Ogege, S.O.; viii, ix, 119
Oghara; 100
Oghenekaro, Canon; 13
Oghwoghwa; 96
Oginibo; 6
Ogiso dynasty; 4
Ogobiri; 96
Ogor; 95, 100
Ohrerhe; 6
Ojaide, T., iii, vii, viii, ix, 1, 10, 20, 10, 113, 138
Okere; 95
Okpan, Arhibo; 16, 133-137
Okpara Elites Association; 16
Okpara Inland; 114, 141
Okpara Waterside; 114
Okpara, 114, 152
Okparabe; 95, 100
Okpare; 106
Okpe; 5, 15, 95, 97, 100, 101, 128
Okurekpo; 114
Okwagbe; 7, 12, 145, 146
Old Oyo; 4
Olomu; 15, 95, 97
Oloya; 13
Ombongi; 144, 145
Ominigbo; 7
Omuofa, Agadaye; 143
Onobrakpeya, Bruce; 17
Onogbo, Ukoko; 141
Onojete, Chief Dickson; 3
Onojete, Power; 141-144
Onokerhoraye, A.C.; 120
Onokpasa, B.; 13
Onoriose, W.; viii, ix, 95
Onose, I.J.; viii, ix, 33, 83
Onosode, Gamaliel; 141
Opland, Jeff; 20, 144, 149
Ora; 4
Orality; 7

Orerokpe; 106
Orhuwherun; 6, 142
Orogun, Evang. B. U.; 130
Orogun; 6, 83, 95, 99, 100, 152
Osei, G.K.; 121, 125
Osiokpa, Omokomoko; 16
Osubele, Ayemenokpe E.; 12, 17, 109
Otan, Ogute; 16
Oteri; 98
Otite, Onigu; 4, 8-10, 13, 20, 83, 86, 96, 103, 119, 120, 127, 128, 131, 149
Otota; 16, 115, 139, 140, 144, 145
Otumara; 6
Oviorie; 141
Owhawha; 5, 145
Pan-Edo group of language; 4
Patani; 96
Performance fees; 143
Pidgin English and Urhobo; 18
Pidgin English; 7
Pike, K.L.; 21
Plosives; 65
Praxis and aesthetics of Urhobo "disco" music; 133
Recent academic progress; 17
Rhotics; 69
Robbins, R.H.; 84, 92
Roscoe, Adrian; 138
Sadjere, G.E.; 83, 93
Salubi, Chief T.E.A.; 106
Salvation in Urhobo religious cosmogony; 119
Sapele; 18, 86, 106, 152
Schiller, Andrew; 99, 103
Shagari, Alh. Shehu; 136
Sharakure, Solomon; 130
Silvoso; 125
Sjogren, S.; 125
Sound system of Urhobo; 63
Special body marks; 8
Spiro, M.E.; 119, 126
Split verbs; 48
"Spraying", 143
Standard Urhobo; 5, 12
Stark, R. and William, S.B.; 119, 126
Stark, R.; 119, 126
Stockwel *et al.*; 53
Storey, J.; 131

Stray, M.P.H.; 53
Syllable structure; 78
Tadafurhe, W.A.; 12
Temporal adverbs; 35
The relative clause; 39
The verbal group; 46
Tisio, of Agbarho; 143
Tisio, of Oviorie; 143
Tone marking in the writing system; 30
Tone system in Urhobo; 21-31
Transitive verbs; 47
Ubuara, Emmanuel London; 145, 146
Udje; 13
Udoji Awards (1974); 135
Udu; 12, 13, 15, 95, 100-102
Uduophori; 98
Ufuoma Club; 16
Ufuoma; 98
Ughelle; 95
Ughelli; 11, 13, 86, 99, 100, 152
Ugheteni, S.S.; 2
Ughievwen; 95, 100
Ughwerun (Uwherun); 97, 100, 152
Ujevwe (kingdom); 12, 13, 15, 146
Ukere; 14, 17, 56
Ukoko r'Etota r'Urhobo; 141
Ukwani; 5, 6, 9, 56, 83, 84, 100, 120
UNESCO; vi, 3
Unoh, S.O.; 91
Urbanisation, impact of; 106
Urhobo dialects; 99
Urhobo Foundation; 109
Urhobo gospel music; 127
Urhobo Historical Society; 17
Urhobo history and European encounter; 10
Urhobo kingdoms; 95
Urhobo Language Committee; 13
Urhobo lexicon; 17
Urhobo myths; 10
Urhobo neighbours; 6
Urhobo orators; 139
Urhobo pastors; 1
Urhobo Progressive Union (UPU); 16, 106, 110
Urhobo proverbs; 113
Urhobo Social Club; 2, 16
Urhobo Studies Programme; 16, 19

Urhobo Voice; 17, 109
Uvwie (Evwron); 5, 13, 15, 95, 102, 128
Uyovukherhi; Atiboroko; 18
Uzere; 128
V syllable; 80
Vowel elision; 74
Vowel harmony in the noun; 77
Vowel harmony in the verbal system; 77
Vowel harmony; 75
Vowel segments; 70
Vowel sequences; 72
WADOO; 17, 109
Warri; 14, 15, 18, 106, 108, 152
Welch, Doris; 99
Welmers, W.E.; 21, 32, 53
Williamson, Kay; 4, 20, 32, 92, 93
Yon'Urhobo; 2
Yule, George; 100, 103
Zulu; 144, 145

www.ingramcontent.com/pod-product-compliance
Lightning Source LLC
Chambersburg PA
CBHW031553300426
44111CB00006BA/294